Unintended Consequences in Singapore

Unintended Consequences in Singapore

Edited by

David Chan
Singapore Management University, Singapore

World Scientific

NEW JERSEY • LONDON • SINGAPORE • BEIJING • SHANGHAI • HONG KONG • TAIPEI • CHENNAI • TOKYO

Published by

World Scientific Publishing Co. Pte. Ltd.
5 Toh Tuck Link, Singapore 596224
USA office: 27 Warren Street, Suite 401-402, Hackensack, NJ 07601
UK office: 57 Shelton Street, Covent Garden, London WC2H 9HE

British Library Cataloguing-in-Publication Data
A catalogue record for this book is available from the British Library.

UNINTENDED CONSEQUENCES IN SINGAPORE

ISBN 978-981-3231-73-3

For any available supplementary material, please visit
https://www.worldscientific.com/worldscibooks/10.1142/10756#t=suppl

Desk Editor: Sandhya Venkatesh

Typeset by Stallion Press
Email: enquiries@stallionpress.com

To all who want to understand
unintended consequences in Singapore
to co-create solutions that
prevent negative outcomes and promote positive ones.

About the Editor

David Chan received his PhD in Industrial and Organizational Psychology from Michigan State University. He is Professor of Psychology and Director of the Behavioural Sciences Institute at the Singapore Management University (SMU). He is a recipient of the Lee Kuan Yew Fellowship Award for Research Excellence. He is also Adjunct Principal Scientist at the Agency for Science, Technology and Research (A*STAR) and Co-Director of the Centre for Technology and Social-Behavioural Insights which is jointly established by A*STAR and SMU. He was formerly Deputy Provost of SMU, Deputy Director of Wharton-SMU Research Centre, and the founding Interim Dean of the SMU School of Social Sciences.

Professor Chan's research includes areas in longitudinal modeling, personnel selection, adaptation to changes at work, and subjective well-being. His works have been published in top psychology, management, and methods journals such as *Applied Psychological Measurement*, *Cognition*, *Current Directions in Psychological Science*, *Human*

Performance, International Review of Industrial and Organizational Psychology, Journal of Applied Psychology, Journal of Personality and Social Psychology, Multivariate Behavioral Research, Organizational Behavior and Human Decision Processes, Organizational Research Methods, Personality and Social Psychology Bulletin, Personnel Psychology, and Professional Psychology: Research and Practice. He has authored or edited 10 books published by Routledge, Sage, and World Scientific in the areas of adaptability, personnel selection, liveability, positivity, social futures, psychological capital, unintended consequences, public trust, and social, political and psychological issues in Singapore.

In 2000, Professor Chan was ranked 9th world-wide in the Top 100 most published researchers of the 1990's in the top journals of Industrial and Organizational Psychology. His works have been cited several thousand times in various disciplines. He has received several international scholarly awards including the Edwin Ghiselli Award for Innovative Research Design, the William Owen Scholarly Achievement Award, and the Distinguished Early Career Contributions Award from the Society for Industrial and Organizational Psychology and the Dissertation Research Award from the American Psychological Association.

He has served as Senior Editor of the *Asia Pacific Journal of Management*, Associate Editor of the *Journal of Organizational Behavior*, Advisory Editor for *Oxford Bibliographies (Management)* published by the Oxford University Press, member on editorial boards of several journals and reviewer for several grant agencies in United States, Hong Kong and Singapore.

Professor Chan is consultant to numerous public and private sector organisations in Singapore; a member of the

Social Science Research Council, the National Council on Problem Gambling (NCPG), the Diabetes Prevention and Care Taskforce, the Singapore-Japan Joint Committee on Science and Technology, and the International Panel of Experts and Research and Development Advisory Panel for the Urban Redevelopment Authority; a director on the Board of the Singapore Corporation of Rehabilitative Enterprises and the Board of the National Volunteer and Philanthropy Centre; and Chairman of the International Advisory Panel to the NCPG & National Addictions Management Service. He has also previously served as a member of Public Hygiene Council, the International Advisory Panel for the SkillsFuture Singapore and the Workforce Singapore, the Governing Board for the Workplace Safety and Health Institute, the Research Advisory Panel for the National Population and Talent Division, and a director on the Board of the Agri-Food and Veterinary Authority.

He is a recipient of the Long Service Volunteer Award and the Outstanding Volunteer Award from the Ministry of Social and Family Development, the Long Service Volunteer Award and the Special Recognition Honour by the Ministry of Home Affairs for outstanding contributions to the Home Team in the field of psychology, and the Public Administration Medal (Silver) which is a National Day Award presented by the President of the Republic of Singapore.

Professor Chan writes op-ed articles in *The Straits Times*' By Invitation Series, which is a regular newspaper column on social issues. He appears regularly on *Channel NewsAsia* current affairs television programmes and he is the consultant to the *Channel NewsAsia*'s "Social

Experiment", which is a 5-part programme series that examines human behaviours and social phenomena using scientific experiments, as well as "Days of Disasters', which is a 5-part documentary series that examines the lessons learned from previous disasters in Singapore.

Together with Nobel Laureate in Economics Professor Daniel Kahneman and Professor Ed Diener, Professor Chan served on an international committee that submitted to the United Nations a report on measures of national well-being across countries. He is the first scientist in the world to receive Elected Fellow status of all six international psychological organisations namely, the American Psychological Association, the Association for Psychological Science, the International Association of Applied Psychology, the Society for Industrial and Organisational Psychology, the Society for Personality and Social Psychology and the American Psychological Association's Division for Personality and Social Psychology.

About the Contributors

David Chan is Professor of Psychology & Director of the Behavioural Sciences Institute at the Singapore Management University and Adjunct Principal Scientist at A*STAR. He has received numerous international awards on scientific contributions and his works have been cited several thousand times in various disciplines. He has served as Editor or board member on numerous journals. He is advisor, consultant or board member to various organisations in the public, private and people sectors both locally and internationally, and the first scientist in the world to receive Elected Fellow status of all six international psychological organisations.

Chan Heng Chee is Ambassador-At-Large at the Ministry of Foreign Affairs, Chairman of the Lee Kuan Yew Centre for Innovative Cities in the Singapore University of Technology and Design and the National Arts Council and a member of the Presidential Council for Minority Rights. She was the founding Director of the Institute of Policy Studies. She has served as Ambassador to the United States and Mexico, Permanent Representative to the United Nations and High Commissioner to Canada. She is recipient of numerous awards from Singapore, Australia, United Kingdom and United States.

Arnoud De Meyer is President of the Singapore Management University. He has a Master of Science in Electrical Engineering, MBA and PhD in Management from the University of Ghent in Belgium. Previously, he was Director of Judge Business School at the University of Cambridge. He has held various senior positions at INSEAD including the founding Dean of INSEAD's Asia Campus in Singapore. He publishes widely in academic journals and books. He has consulted for organisations in Europe and Asia and serves as board member for various organisations in Singapore.

Han Fook Kwang is Editor-at-Large at The Straits Times, Singapore Press Holdings Ltd and a Senior Fellow at the S Rajaratnam School of International Studies, Nanyang Technological University. He spent 10 years in the Administrative Service before joining The Straits Times in 1989. He was Editor of the paper from 2002 to 2012. He is a Board member of the Building and Construction Authority. He graduated from the University of Leeds and also holds a Masters in Public Administration from Harvard University.

Tommy Koh is Ambassador-At-Large at the Ministry of Foreign Affairs, Special Adviser of the Institute of Policy Studies, Chairman of the Centre for International Law and Rector of Tembusu College at the National University of

Singapore, and Chairman of the SymAsia Foundation of Credit Suisse. He was Singapore's Permanent Representative to the United Nations in New York and Ambassador to the United States. He was also the Chief Negotiator for the USA-Singapore Free Trade Agreement. He has served as the United Nation Secretary-General's Special Envoy to Russia, Estonia, Latvia and Lithuania.

Jeremy Lim is Partner and Head, Health and Life Sciences Practice, Asia Pacific, Oliver Wyman. He has held different senior executive positions in both private and public sector organisations, including in the Ministry of Health. A medical doctor by training, he holds a Masters in public health degree from the Johns Hopkins School of Public Health and a Masters in medicine (surgery) from the National University of Singapore. He is author of a book on the Singapore healthcare system.

Lim Lai Cheng is Executive Director of the SMU Academy at the Singapore Management University. Prior to joining the university, she had worked as teacher, head of department, deputy principal and principal at three schools. She has served on various national committees on education reviews in Singapore. She is a Director of the Principals' Academy, Inc. (Singapore) and advisor to several education foundations in Sweden, Slovakia, South Africa and Russia.

Kishore Mahbubani is Senior Advisor (University & Global Relations) and Professor in the Practice of Public Policy at the National University of Singapore. He served for over three decades in Singapore's diplomatic service including as the Permanent Secretary for Foreign Affairs,

Singapore's Permanent Representative to the United Nations, and the President of the United Nations Security Council. He has published in a wide range of journals and newspapers, and his books have been translated widely. He has received numerous international recognitions such as being selected by various magazines in their lists of top global thinkers.

Mathew Mathews is a Senior Research Fellow at the Institute of Policy Studies. Previously, he was a faculty member at the Department of Sociology at the National University of Singapore. His research includes those on race, religion and immigrant integration as well as issues related to family, ageing and poverty. He has served as consultant for several research projects in government agencies and is active in community service. He is a Research Advisor to the Ministry of Social and Family Development.

Neo Boon Siong is the Dean and Canon Professor of Business of the Nanyang Business School at the Nanyang Technological University. He is a Fellow of the Civil Service College, Centre for Liveable Cities and Health Leadership College. He has published widely in research areas in business strategy and information technology management. He serves as board member on numerous organisations in the public and private sectors. He has advised many major government institutions and business corporations in the areas of governance, business strategy, process management and organisational change.

Paulin Straughan is Dean of Students and Professor of Sociology (Practice) at the Singapore Management

University. Her research interests are in marriage, parenthood, ageing and other areas in the sociology of family and medical sociology. She has received numerous teaching awards. She has served as a consultant on survey projects for several government agencies and was a Nominated Member of Parliament from 2009 to 2011.

Tan Kok Yam is Deputy Secretary (Strategy Group) and Head of the Smart Nation Programme Office at the Prime Minister's Office. Previously, he had served in the Ministry of Defence, the Ministry of National Development and the Ministry of Education. He is an engineer by training, having graduated from the University College London in 1997 with a Bachelor in Electrical and Electronic Engineering and a Master of Science in Telecommunications. He also completed the one-year Sloan Program at the Stanford Graduate School of Business as a Fulbright Scholar.

Preface

When policymakers, communities or advocates make decisions and take actions, they do so with the purpose of achieving some desired goal. But sometimes, unintended consequences occur. These are outcomes that are not the ones intended by the purposeful decision or action. Unintended consequences can be positive or negative, although the discussions often focus on the unexpected adverse impact that may result from well-intentioned policies or public actions.

It is tempting to say that unintended consequences happen because we live in an uncertain and unpredictable world, and that there is not much we can do to prevent their occurrence or prepare for them. In fact, many unintended consequences are neither predetermined nor random. It is true that whether or not unintended consequences happen will be affected by many economic and social factors that Singapore is confronted with, but much will also depend on how we approach these factors and the potential consequences.

This book, based on the proceedings at the Behavioural Sciences Institute Conference 2017, explores various issues about unintended consequences in Singapore. The book is organised into four parts. Part 1 provides an overview of issues involved in thinking about unintended consequences. Part 2 examines unintended consequences in the context of Singapore's goal to become a smart nation and compares the perspectives between public and private sector organisations on dealing with uncertainty. Part 3 analyses the relationships linking unintended consequences to healthcare outcomes and the management of race relations in Singapore. Part 4 addresses specific questions on unintended consequences in Singapore in terms of the nation's history, immigration, education, meritocracy, civil service culture and mindsets, and relationships between people and government.

This book will provide the reader new perspectives and possibilities related to achieving intended societal goals and building a strong Singapore society.

Professor David Chan
Director, Behavioural Sciences Institute
Singapore Management University

Contents

Part I

Chapter 1

An Innovative Singapore in an Uncertain World: Dealing with Unknowns and Unintended Consequences

Arnoud De Meyer

Good morning to all of you, and a very warm welcome to BSI Conference 2017. Looking at the theme of this conference, I must admit that a casual conversation with David sometime in November led to one unintended consequence, which was that I have to deliver an entire speech here today. I am not sure if I will directly speak to the issues of unintended consequences in Singapore, but I will develop a related theme in my talk, which is that Singapore now lives in a very different world, and there will be intended and unintended consequences. The world is a lot more uncertain and Singapore is a very different place than what it was, say 15 years ago. We are now in a world where we need to innovate more, and the question I wish to address is whether we are prepared for that.

Let me first reflect on the differences between the issues facing the CFE (Committee for the Future of the Economy) in 2017 and those faced by the national committee formed 15 years ago, which I had the honour and pleasure to be part of, when we looked at what was needed then in 2001. I think there were five ways that the world has transformed in the last 15 years. *These are: digital (from information scarcity to overload), environmental (from abundant resources to need for utilization control), economic (from globalisation to mercantilism), social (from measured optimism to sense of loss of control), and geographical (from West to East).*

First, we each have a view on what digital transformation is. But it is a little bit like the elephant that is touched by a number of blind people. That is, for some people, an elephant is a leg; and for others, it may be the teeth, or whatever. We do not have an exact model of what the digital world is all about. From my perspective, the most important issue is that we have moved from the world with a high level of information scarcity to a world with information abundance or even information overload. I noticed this as a professor at SMU (Singapore Management University). I compare our students today with myself when I was a university student, which of course was a very long time ago. I remember queuing up at libraries to get access to the latest issue of a journal that was particularly relevant for me, making photocopies of the journal articles. And as students we were sort of competing with each other to get access to the information. Libraries then had almost a monopoly on information. We now live in a very different world. To give you the example of SMU, we still have a physical library but we have far fewer books in there. We have about 58,000 physical printed books but we have more than 390,000 online books, and our students have access to a wealth of information including a wide range of databases.

So, the world is moving fast with digital transformation. Information is available, and there is for many of us an information overload. The problem with information overload is that we are often either paralysed because we have too much information, or that we used the wrong information. One of the things we need to do with our young students is to help them understand how to differentiate between the good, the bad, and the ugly when it comes to information. As academics, we knew that before it became fashionable to talk about alternative facts or fake news.

The second big change for the world is the environmental transformation. The world I came from 40 years ago was one where resources were abundant and unlimited. I still remember that in my undergraduate course on economics, air and water were described as free goods. Today, and we can look at Budget 2017, water is definitely not a free good anymore. So we have moved from a world with abundant resources to one with very limited resources. We now have to think a lot more about how to control the utilisation of those resources.

The third transformation is the economic transformation. The world in 2001 believed in globalisation. There were practically no voices that would say that globalisation was bad. That has become very different today. You only have to see what happens under the new administration in the United States. But that is only the tip of the iceberg. The doubts about or the challenge of globalisation is an important one. A number of economists have noted the negative consequences of globalisation, such as the rising gap between rich and poor or the geographic dislocation of production. These negative consequences have led us to review our ideas about globalisation.

The fourth transformation is the social transformation. My sense is that back then in 2001 there was actually quite a lot of optimism. I would say "measured optimism", in the sense that, while not everything was perfect, we not only knew that the world was improving but we actually were seeing that the world was improving. I am not sure about Singapore, but based on what I read, and based on my travels to Europe and United States, it has become very clear to me that a large part of the population elsewhere have now doubts on whether they are still progressing. Don't misunderstand me. The facts are still showing that the world is much better off today than it was 15 years ago. There are far less poor people now. We actually have less people die in wars or through terrorism than through suicides. In other words, the number of people dying from state conflicts or from guerrilla movements has been reduced not only proportionally to the world population but also in absolute terms. So, factually, we live in a better world, but there may not be that perception among large groups of the world's population. So I think there is a social transformation from what I call a measured optimism towards a world where many sense of loss of control.

Finally, we all know about the geographical transformation. By this, I mean that the point of gravity of economic activity is gradually moving from West to East. We see that in the growth of Singapore but also in our surrounding countries in South East Asia, China and others. It is now a very different world.

If we look at the past 15 years, we see that Singapore has also changed to a more mature economy. Economically, we have moved from mainly serving Japan, Europe and United States to now having a set of strong local sectors such as advanced manufacturing, logistics, financial services, petro-chemicals, health management and tourism. The report of the CFE also spoke about deepening these sectors rather than inventing new ones. The report was about deepening the capabilities through industry transformation maps for the different sectors.

At the same time, Singapore now has global visibility, due to brilliant marketing of the city. People know about Singapore — not just about Formula One, but also about what Singapore stands for.

Of course, there are also changes in Singapore demographics, and we are a maturing society with people of greater longevity. Notice that I said "longevity", which is about living longer and being able to do many interesting things, and not "ageing", which I consider to be a negative word.

Singapore also has the ambition to be one of the world's "buzziest" cities. By that I mean a city where there is the buzz in the society, with many activities in terms of arts, culture, sports, tourism and whatever else we can think of. This Singapore city is a very different one from 15 years ago.

However, there are limits to Singapore's growth due to limits in physical land and infrastructure, people, capabilities, and soft power. Can we do as a country of five-and-a-half million people? We cannot be a jack-of-all-trades. So we need to focus; we need to understand what we are good at and what we are not doing, and understand the limits of some of the soft power that Singapore had developed and so on.

So what that it is a very new Singapore? Well, it is a very new Singapore in a very different world. The problem is that the set of examples that we had and that we could copy previously, is no longer the same now. Look around to see where we can learn something from the rest of the world. The set of examples is not empty, and it is not an old set, but the examples are drying up. There are not that many countries or cities anymore that we can go to and ask how we would learn from them, and adapt for example our educational system, or adapt our social security, healthcare system, and so on. Indeed, we see that there are no silver bullets in the CFE report. There are no totally new ideas or initiatives like the way we came up with an integrated resort or life sciences or global schoolhouses. It is all about deepening what we do well and doing it better.

From my perspective, we need to invest more in what I call the soft aspect of the economy, and not just the hard infrastructure, building new factories, building new roads, and putting in fiberglass cables for the digital economy. Yes, we still need to keep doing all those and renew our infrastructure and build the hard infrastructure of the economy. But at the same time, we will have to invest a lot more in that uncertain area of the types of soft skills and deep skills that the economy needs, which also includes skills on entrepreneurship. We need to develop our capabilities for design, and build the global networks and global innovation alliances that the CFE report talked about.

Business model innovation is one of the key concepts in the report of the CFE. — Here, I want to emphasise that we need to have more and better social and behavioural sciences research to support the development of business models. The keyword for me is innovation. It is not that we did not do innovation previously. But I do think that one of the anticipated consequences of the big changes that Singapore and the world is going or has gone through, whether intended or unintended, is that we will have to be innovative in a different way.

Now, the question to ask then is: Are we good as an innovation hub? Are we able to be that innovation hub for the world? That is an area in which I have done much research in. In my earlier days from 2000 to 2010, I studied many innovation hubs including the Silicon Valley and what was happening in Tel Aviv, in Munich, in Sweden, or in the area of biosciences around Cambridge in United Kingdom. I also looked at others, such as in Taiwan where there were some very successful industrial parks. My research conclusion is that you need to invest in six major areas to be an innovation hub. These are (1) a robust and performing technical infrastructure, (2) strength and depth of human capital, (3) an appropriate legal framework, (4) financial engineers who can accompany the innovators, (5) respect and rewards for creativity, and (6) access to markets. Let me say a few words about each of these areas.

A robust and performing technical infrastructure includes our universities. Of course, universities are not purely technical. But what I am highlighting is the universities' capabilities in research and development. It is important to continue to invest in the university infrastructures such as laboratories and fibre optics.

As for the strength and the depth of human capital, it does not only refer to the PhD graduates and top-quality researchers we need. We also need very good laboratory technicians, as well as marketing people who can help commercialise some of the research results. So the strength and depth of human capital is about the whole education system in Singapore.

Obviously, we need an appropriate legal framework for innovation to work. By a legal framework, I mean the need to be able to protect and trade our intellectual property, and we need to be able to enforce contracts.

We need to have the financial engineers who can accompany the innovators. We need to have the people that can mobilise the resources so that we can actually commercialise some of the innovative ideas. We need to have that absorptive capacity of the economy to take on the great ideas and translate them to effective businesses.

We need to have respect and reward for creative ideas. Perhaps, we need students who pursue a creative career that does not follow the standard career pathway. Here, we need to have role models of creative people who show how you can be successful by being a designer or by coming up with a crazy idea and translating it into a business or a service.

Finally, we need to have access to markets. We need to have markets that can absorb some of these creative ideas. One of the big advantages of the Silicon Valley is that it has the entire United States as its home market. And for Tel Aviv, its advantage is not that it has a big market. In fact, it has a market that is probably smaller than Singapore because it has difficulties exporting ideas to its neighbouring countries. But what it has is very good relationships with people in the United States. So what is happening is that the home market for Tel Aviv is very often New York, Philadelphia, Boston, the Midwest, and California.

Now, where do Singapore stand? Of course, we may all disagree on the answer, but let me attempt to project a hypothesis on how we are doing on these six areas. First, I would say we are quite outstanding when it comes to having an appropriate legal framework. I would actually put us at the top of the scale in this area. We have a very good legal framework in which we can operate. Second, while we may sometimes complain about our education systems, we do know that our educational system is actually quite good in comparison to most other industrialised countries in the world. Again, I would give our education, which relates to the strength and depth of human capital, almost a full score here. Although of course we need to continue to improve.

Perhaps I am exaggerating a bit here when I also give the highest evaluation to our technical infrastructure. We have an advantage here, with Singapore being a country and a city at the same time.

So I would say on these three areas namely, legal framework, education, and infrastructure, I give it a very high ranking.

I would say access to markets is our problem. We are far away from sophisticated markets. But having said that, we are perhaps very often neglecting the close-by markets. Indonesia, a very large market, is at our doorsteps but we sometimes neglect it. When I ask students in my class how many provinces does Indonesia have, nobody seems to know the answer. Why are we so ignorant about our neighbour? We have a large and wonderful market just next door and we do not know too much about it. So some of the lack of access to markets is self-imposed. Vietnam is another large and nearby market.

With regard to the role models and innovation culture, I think it is improving. Compared to say fifteen years ago, students now are more prepared to set up a company, when they have some creative ideas. And this is now less likely to be considered as a failure or not a real job by their parents or relatives. And in terms of sophisticated risk financing, we are now very good in start-ups and there is a lot of funding available through various government schemes and proof-of-concept subsidies. Our banks are very good at helping large companies but what is lacking is growth capital. Once you have started up, we need to help the company to grow. And that is the reason why I am very optimistic about start-ups and entrepreneurship in Singapore, but not so optimistic about having real growth of companies. It seems that many of the startups will go overseas and try to figure out where they can get the financial support to grow.

So, overall, Singapore is not too bad at all. None of the innovation hubs in the world are perfect. All of them are successful because they score outstandingly on some dimensions while they are good enough on others. I think Singapore, as an innovation hub, has a lot going for itself. But on top of the things that we have put in place for a great innovation hub, including the good legal framework and education system, and financing, role models and entrepreneurship will get better, it requires a little more.

Singapore needs to develop a passion to innovate. We need to have more people with enough passion to be disrupters and go against the accepted ways of doing things. That means we need to tolerate messiness and creative chaos. We also need to accept diversity, not only racial and religious diversity, but also the diversity and differences in opinions. It is out of interaction and differences in ideas that often emerge creative insights. We also need to realise that we live in a world that is constantly changing. Within that dynamic world, Singapore has to constantly reposition itself. Finally, we need to make choices and focus on selected trades rather than all trades. I have a lot of admiration for what I read in the CFE report. But I was surprised when I saw that there will be twenty-three industry transformation maps. For a country of five million people, that is one industry transformation map per 200,000. Is that realistic?

To conclude, I would say that if we want to do well, it also requires taking a different approach to project and programme management. About ten years ago I wrote a book about "managing the unknown", which was about project management when you are confronted with a high level of uncertainty. What we said in that book is similar to what Minister Heng Swee Keat said in the quote that David showed us this morning. That is, when there is limited uncertainty in the world, we can use traditional programme management, or what we call the instructionist approach. We have a plan and we follow the plan in the implementation. But when we are working under high uncertainty and complexity, we need a learning and adaptive approach that involves focusing on many small projects at the same time. We need to be very flexible and pragmatic. So maybe that is the reason why there are twenty-three industry transformation maps. We will see which ones work, which few ones will survive and succeed. But we will need to be able to say we have many projects at the same time, and we will cull some of them, if necessary, at the right time. We must be willing to cut our losses and consolidate our learning.

Thank you very much.

Chapter 2

Approaches to Unintended Consequences in Singapore

David Chan

A very good morning to all. Similar to our previous BSI conferences, my presentation will try to set the stage for the discussions in various sessions in this conference. I will provide an overview of the issues that I think matter in the notion of unintended consequences. Some of the ideas that I will be sharing with you may be general and therefore somewhat vague, but I hope it will help you think through some of the issues as they emerge in the subsequent sessions. As the title of my talk indicates, I will organise the issues in terms of approaches to unintended consequences.

If you look up the dictionaries, check out various books or search online, you will not find a consensus or even a clear definition for the meaning of unintended consequences. I think there are reasons for this, which I will share with you later in my talk. But to begin our discussion on the same page, I have constructed my own working definition, which is as follows.

"An unintended consequence refers to the occurrence of a specific set of results, situation or state of affairs that was not the outcome intended by a purposeful action but was brought about by the action."

It is important to think through these various characteristics in the definition. We are referring to the occurrence of some specific set of results and not just how things are in general. And the results are about a situation or state of affairs that was not the outcome that was intended by a purposive action, but it was brought about by that action. That means we are not talking about some behaviours like random or reflex actions that you did without thinking and then something happened due to the action. The action that led to the unintended consequences was a purposeful action. The purpose was a particular intended outcome. What has actually happened now is not that intended outcome, but it must be somehow linked to the action. In other words, the actual outcome occurred because of your purposive action — your action either somehow contributed or directly caused the consequence that was not the intended outcome. It is important to bring these different ideas together, so we do not end up saying that unintended consequences are just anything and everything that we do not like, or like. When we define or conceptualise unintended consequences in the way that I just did, it sets the stage for a useful discussion, for both the policymakers and the people who criticise or evaluate a policy.

Let me begin by sharing with you some well-known real examples of unintended consequences. These examples illustrate several general points. As we think through these examples and general points, we can try to relate them to our personal life, our social life, our family, and also our group dynamics and issues at the workplace. And of course, we can link it to policymaking. Many of the examples are actually about public policies.

The first story I want to tell you is about toads and pests in Australian cane fields. Some of you may have heard this true story. In some parts of Australia, there was a serious problem of a huge population of Cane Toads found in the suburbs. The irony is that the toads were first introduced as an intervention to deal with another cane infestation problem caused by a pest known as the Cane beetles. Unfortunately, the toad solution did not work. The toads ended up eating many things except the beetles. And the toads were prolific in reproduction. So very soon you get a large toad population in the fields and outside as well. The action intended to solve a pest problem ended up with two pests. This is an example of intended consequences that we are familiar with in our personal and work lives. You intended to solve a problem and the unintended consequence was that, not only that it did not work, your solution became the second problem and the first problem remains. By the way, many of our problems are like pests, where one plus one is often more than two.

Now, the story of the cobras. In colonial India, the British government wanted to solve the problem of free-roaming cobras, which were posing a danger to the public. The government officials thought of a solution. They decided to offer a monetary reward to any local who brings in a dead cobra. It appeared to work — many dead snakes were presented and so the reward money were given out. But soon, the government found out that people were breeding cobras to get the reward money, and they dutifully ended the programme. Left with worthless cobras, the locals released them into the wild. The policy had cost a small fortune; and instead of reducing the cobra population, the bounty probably increased it. Our policymakers need to pay attention here. Financial incentive is not always the correct solution. Do not just give out money as a reward to produce all kinds of behaviours that you want to encourage. You may produce a cobra effect.

A similar situation occurred in Vietnam, in Hanoi, when it was under French rule. What the British did to the Indians, the French did to the Vietnamese, except this time it was a rat problem and not cobras. The similar unintended consequence of the reward was that the people started farming rats. But there is an interesting difference in this rat story. The French said please don't bring me the entire dead rat. Just bring me the rat's tail as proof that you killed the rat. So there were tails coming in and rewards were going out. But when the French later started to check, just like your audit from the AGO (Auditor-General's Office), they found many rats roaming around without tails. Obviously, what happened was the people actually cut off the rat's tail without killing it so that the rats can go back and breed more rats for more tails to be harvested. So the people get a continuous supply of rat tails to get the bounty and you ended up with many more rats than before. I know it's a gross story, and you won't want to go around repeating this tale of the rat's tail. But I have now reinforced in you the idea of unintended consequences.

The point here is you can replace the cobra or rat with your favourite policy object. And in Singapore where giving financial incentives seems to be a common policy strategy to try get a target behavior from people or an intended outcome, it is not difficult to think about policies with a cobra effect, or a rat or toad effect. You know, the British and French are smart people too, not very different from our policymakers in Singapore, so intelligence is no guarantee against policy actions that lead to unintended consequences. Note that almost always, the outcome is a more severe problem than before the reward was instituted. That means you wasted taxpayers' money not just by spending it without solving the problem — you created a larger one after stopping the reward, and you had to stop the reward when it was not solving the problem.

Enough of animals. Let's go to seat belts and cyclists, which are famous examples in economics that I want to share here so you appreciate the different aspects and manifestations of unintended consequences. The findings are controversial, and you need not believe them, but my purpose is to illustrate what has been called the "Peltzman Effect". This is the purported pattern of results showing that the number of accidents actually increased after introducing some road safety measures such as mandatory seat belts in vehicles or cycle helmets. The explanation is that the users ended up taking greater risk and believing that they are immune or at least overestimated the protection from the safety device they were using. Never mind if you believe their findings or not about increased accidents. The important point is the introduction of a safety measure can sometimes lead to risk compensation effects where people ended up engaging in more risky behaviours than they should because they underestimated the risks as a result of adopting the safety measure. Of course, you should still wear your seat belts and cycling helmets, simply because they protect you when accidents happen. This by the way illustrates an important point where the presence of an unintended consequence does not always mean we should stop the action. We have to consider and weigh the positive consequences of the action as well. So it is a trade-offs situation that policymakers always talk about, which I will elaborate later.

Policies or programmes that backfire need not be in the form of an incentive. In the United States, a number of states enforce the three-strikes laws, where individuals who already have two prior convictions can be given a very severe prison sentence upon being convicted for a third time, even if the third offence is relatively minor. Studies showed that, instead of acting as a deterrent, enforcing three-strikes laws was linked to an increase in violent crime, especially against law enforcement officers. Apparently this unintended consequence occurred because criminals have a lot to lose, and thus fought violently not to be arrested, especially for a third time. So when you blindly apply a rule like this, you can actually cause injury to your own people.

The Streisand Effect, named after singer Barbara Streisand in an incident in 2003, is another example that many of us will find familiar because of the nature of the Internet. Streisand took legal action to sue a website and try to suppress the posting on the Internet some photographs of her house in California. The action ended up generating more public interest, and the images of her house on Internet were downloaded and viewed by many. So, what happens when you try to suppress something? Well, your action will generate more interest when none existed initially, so it backfires. Here is something that our media regulatory authorities need to understand. Not that you should not have censorship, but sometimes an action to prevent access to a material ended up giving it publicity and more viewership. This relates to the notion of forbidden fruit. The more you forbid something, the more interest, desirability and temptation you may end up creating.

There are many more examples of unintended consequences that happen to us all the time in our personal and work lives.

Those of you working with your departmental budgets think that if you are thrifty and don't spend your budget by the end of the financial year, you end up with unused funds and it may mean you get a lower budget for your next financial year based on your past expenditure because those making budget allocation is also trying to be prudent. You quickly spend all the remaining funds, on things that you may not need, and ended up wasting money.

Then there are many examples of how when we try to increase performance by giving an external or extrinsic reward for something that is actually by itself intrinsically interesting. You end up demotivating the person, because the person now associates the activity with the external reward. This unintended consequence, which Singapore parents and policymakers have much experience because we are always using incentive-based external rewards to increase performance in all domains, whether it is employee performance or our children's performance in academics or intrinsically motivating activities such as playing the piano. This psychological phenomenon, where a person's intrinsic motivation in an activity can be removed when you provide an extrinsic reward for its performance, is quite well established. We need to guard against this — spending money to reward with intent to increase performance, and ending up killing the intrinsic interest and motivation to perform.

Many of the examples that I have given you are what economists called perverse effects, where not only the goal or intended outcome did not materialise, an unintended negative outcome directly opposite to the intended outcome occurred as a result of the goal-directed purposive action. Cobra effects in unintended policy outcomes are clear examples. These effects, which the layperson will say "it backfires", are what most have focused on in the area of public policy, and we will too in this conference, to understand some of these unintended consequences in Singapore.

But let me also highlight that perverse effect is just one of at least three kinds of unintended consequences. In many policy situations of unintended consequences, especially in Singapore, it is more the second kind, which is what we call unexpected drawback. This means that the intended positive outcome, or at least some parts of it, did in fact occur; but at the same time some unintended negative outcome also happened. Peltzman effects from the safety examples, and the examples of intrinsic motivation in an activity decreased by giving external rewards, are unexpected drawbacks. This is because the purposive action led to intended positive outcomes and negative unintended negative outcomes, both at the same time. This is an important point because it directly affects the evaluation of the action or policy, including whether the policy should continue and possibly how to prevent, mitigate or remove the negative outcomes and increase the positive outcomes rather than simply stopping or forgoing the policy. Some will say it is a trade-off situation. This is true sometimes but not all the time. We need to be careful that not every difficult policy situation should be a trade-offs decision-making situation. Otherwise we end up uncritically accepting that negative consequences of policy are always necessary or inevitable and that it is something that we have to accept as a given. I have elaborated on this point extensively in my previous presentations and writings, where I explained paradoxical policymaking that helps us learn to see how two positive goals that appear seemingly opposite may in fact be complementary and can be achieved at the same time.

When discussing unexpected drawback, it is important to highlight that the existence of unintended negative consequences for a policy does not necessarily mean that the policy is inherently flawed or should not be implemented. The larger point here is that translations from policy intent to content to outcome are often not straightforward.

The third kind of unintended consequences, which has received relatively less attention when applied to policymaking, is positive unexpected benefit. This is about a policy outcome that is still unintended and in fact not expected by the policymaker, but it occurred and it is positive. The idea of positive multiplier effects, where positive outcomes that are distinct from the intended outcome of the policy action but occurred because of the action, is a very powerful one that deserves more attention from policymakers and researchers in unintended consequences. It is important to not think that unintended consequences can only be negative.

That unintended consequences can be either negative or positive, that it can either hurt or help, is just one of several aspects of the current narrative of unintended consequences in Singapore that we should revise. For example, we tend to say, or assume, that unintended consequences occur because of unpredictability in a VUCA world. This term VUCA, which has been in use by many in the past decade, is the idea that because the world is volatile, uncertain, complex and ambiguous, we will not be able to predict events and outcomes. So a VUCA world seems a good reason for policymakers to believe or invoke when unintended consequences from policies happen. I certainly don't disagree that the world is VUCA, but I would caution against using it as the sole or even primary reason to understand or explain unintended consequences. I would say that unintended consequences are not predetermined and neither are they random. It is within our control to some extent and we have to plan for it. To say that it is due to a VUCA world is really making an external causal attribution, which I don't think policymaker should do. Now, this does not change the fact in any way that the world is VUCA. But it brings the policymakers back into the picture as an important driver of change and to plan for and influence the outcomes of policies.

Another narrative that unintended consequences are unanticipated. This needs revision. The fact is unintended consequences can either be unanticipated or anticipated.

Unintended consequences is not all about those surprising black swans that are impossible to predict or anticipate. In fact, I would argue that many, and probably most, of the unintended consequences of policies in Singapore are not unanticipated. Why? Because policies in Singapore are typically rolled out only after detailed analyses and robust internal discussions.

Let me explain more and give some examples of how unintended consequences need not always be unanticipated, since most people equate unintended with unanticipated and use them interchangeably. I will also share with you some practical implications when we make the distinction between unintended and unanticipated.

Our Singapore Government has very smart people in policymaking, both politicians and civil servants, and they always engage in a lot of internal discussions and analysis before arriving at a policy decision. Thus, in the course of the deliberations, they would have considered potential unintended consequences, even though the extent would depend on specifics of the situation such as the political direction, the time urgency, the relationships with other policies or people and agencies involved. In other words, the unintended consequence that actually occurred could well have been part of or similar to the set of unintended consequences considered by the policymakers during the deliberations. The fact that they occurred was actually not a surprise to the policymakers, even though they might not have expected or predicted the extent of the problem associated with them.

In other words, practically all policies in Singapore have gone through lots of internal discussions prior to policy decision, design and sometimes execution. It does not mean the policies are all great and wonderful. What it means is that it is entirely plausible, and in fact quite likely, that when intended negative consequences resulted from the policy, those consequences, at least its nature (i.e., what it is about), were in fact already anticipated by the policymakers prior to policy decision.

Why then the policymakers still decided on the policy knowing the unintended negative consequences, you may ask. The answer is often quite simple. And that is because they made an assessment or judgment, after considering the possible and likely positive and negative consequences in totality, that the net effect is still a positive one. Of course, they hoped the negatives would not happen, or that the extent of the impact is not too large to handle.

Take, for example, Singapore's population policies. The policies have, over the years, allowed many foreigners into the country, putting a heavy burden on infrastructure and provoking discontent among Singaporeans. It is quite implausible to say that no one in Government and the civil service has considered or raised the issue of overcrowding and other social issues that may lead to public discontent. The negative consequences must have been considered and weighed against the policy benefits, and the conclusion was a net positive after prioritising issues including economic considerations, which led to trade-offs decision-making where the policy decision was considered justified. Clearly, policymakers did not want any of the negative consequences to occur, so they were unintended by the purposive policy action, but they were not unanticipated. The issue in the population case was that the extent of the problem was underestimated.

When unintended consequences that were not unanticipated occur, there are important implications for public communication and engagement. If policymakers said they were unanticipated, the public may either think policymakers are incompetent or think they are not telling the truth, and so there will be erosion of trust in competence, integrity or benevolence. But if they acknowledge that the negative consequences, like crowding, were anticipated, that might have political costs as the public may think that their social well-being were unimportant to policymakers, even though the policymakers were concerned with citizen economic well-being and had made a judgment based on probability assessments and trade-offs.

So what to do? For good governance, policymaking, public engagement and social compact between people and Government, I strongly suggest that policymakers publicly acknowledge that some of the unintended negative consequences were anticipated but they were underestimated. Not only that — policymakers should explain why and how. It is important to be honest and transparent about the thought process behind policies. In that way, the public is more likely to recognise that the government was making purposive choices among some alternatives, and that it chose to make a trade-off with the good intentions of overall citizen well-being. The entire situation then becomes meaningful even though it may still be unpleasant, and it may reduce widespread propagation of conspiracy theories and prevent conspiratory beliefs from taking root.

This acknowledgment and explanation will still carry some political cost because governments can no longer attribute the unintended consequences to external factors beyond their control. Because you anticipated it, you now have to justify your choice and be accountable for it. But I think this is a better approach than letting everybody blame you for unintended consequences that they think were unanticipated, which will surely lead to erosion of trust in all dimensions.

When it comes to communication with the public and public engagement, it is important for policymakers to understand Psychology 101 on how people make causal attributions when they observe or experience an outcome. This basic knowledge will help make sense of public reactions, help prevent negative reactions and promote positive ones.

Now, the unintended consequences or outcomes can be either positive or negative, and we can then examine the causal attributions of the outcomes made by policymakers versus the public, which are basically their answers to why the unintended consequences happened. From the well-established research findings in the psychology of causal attribution, we can expect public perception to differ significantly from policymakers' perceptions or beliefs. For example, policymakers may choose to blame negative unintended consequences on an unpredictable world — remember the VUCA world explanation. But the public — especially when they do not understand the trade-offs involved — is more likely to blame the government for being incompetent or dishonest. Conversely, policymakers may choose to credit a serendipitous or positive unintended consequence to good policy design and execution. But the public is more likely to attribute it to luck, or to take the view that a government with ample resources should be expected to produce such results.

Policymakers need to understand these causal attribution tendencies. Plan and prepare for them so that public engagement can be more effective and not be taken by surprise of backlash when unintended consequences happen. I suggest that policymakers be quite explicit to themselves and to the public about the positions they take in policymaking. What matters to the public is that they see that policymakers understand their needs and concerns, but also their perspectives and perceptions. Ultimately, it is perspectives and perceptions that drive how the public thinks, feels and acts, which in turn affect public trust. Public trust can be easily eroded by unintended consequences. And it will not be mitigated by policymakers telling the public that they did not want or did not expect the consequences to happen.

Let me conclude with a few P's, which are habits for policymakers to avoid or develop, to effectively deal with unintended consequences. They may look obvious as principles, but are often neglected in practice.

When communicating their policies to the public, policymakers cannot afford to let themselves be perceived or labelled as perplexed, populist, paranoid, patronising or parochial. These P's are "maladaptive" traits that will only provoke discontent and distrust among the public. Instead, policymakers must take adaptive approaches when dealing with unintended consequences. They should understand that it is possible to proactively prevent some negative unintended consequences, while at the same time aspiring to promote positive ones. A paradoxical approach to policymaker needs to be factored in because not every difficult policy situation needs to be a trade-offs situation. Seemingly opposite goals may not be inherently contradictory. It is possible to have a vibrant economy and high social cohesion, (including good local-foreigner relations) in Singapore. There is no reason why a strong economy and a strong society cannot co-exist. Finally, in order to adapt to unintended consequences, it is important for policymakers to be more pluralistic and people-centric when dealing with different ideas including those that they may not agree, whether initially or after discussion. Of course, all these should be rooted and implemented in a principled and pragmatic way.

Ultimately, remember no one has all the answers. At the end of the day, we need to guard against complacency and our own confirmatory biases, and learn to be open to ideas and see things from others' perspectives. When we can do this, we will develop a strong and sustainable social compact between people and Government, based on mutual trust. With that, we can all approach and deal with unintended consequences in a much better way.

Thank you very much.

Chapter 3

Panel Discussion 1

Panelists: Arnoud De Meyer, David Chan
Moderator: Han Fook Kwang

Fook Kwang: Let me start with you, Arnoud, in the order of the presentation. You spoke about innovation. Some people are of the view that, in the past when Singapore was a newly emerging independent country with very few resources, we were more risk-taking because we had to do certain things. Whereas today, because we have been so successful and we have lots more resources, we have a lot more to lose if we make mistakes. Therefore, we are more risk adverse, especially in the area of public policy. What is your view on this?

Arnoud: It is an interesting question, and I am almost tempted to say yes on the one hand and no on the other hand. I think that you are right that because of the assets that Singapore has built up (and I do not mean necessarily all the physical assets; but also the sort of the intangibles assets such as the harmony in the country and the capabilities and skills of the people) that actually when we make a mistake as a country in policy, the consequences, unintended or intended, or as David noted, anticipated or not anticipated, that the consequences are usually much more important. If you are in a small developing country like Singapore fifty years ago, you try out the policy and if it does not work, you can quite quickly adapt and the losses are relatively low. So yes, since we have a lot more to lose, since we have built up so many tangible and intangible assets, people naturally become more cautious and probably think through more what could be the implications of what they are doing.

On the other hand, I feel that within this relatively protected environment, the students with whom I interact, including both student in the class I teach and many I work with as the President, are actually more willing to take risks. Let me give you an example. At our university, we have an incubator where we have small budding entrepreneurial initiatives of some of our students. Every year, we have around eighty applications for that. Now, we are a relatively small university, and eighty groups of students are willing to set up their small company and not follow the pre-determined way that their parents probably would love. So my answer to your question is partially yes, because as a policymaker, as a government, and as an institution, we are all a little bit more risk adverse because we have more to lose. But the individuals who work in it for themselves are probably willing to take more risks. So I am giving a bit of a paradoxical answer.

Fook Kwang: Thank you, Arnoud. Let me now go to you, David. Unintended consequences is a very wide subject, and you have given us some incredibly good examples. But can I be more specific about Singapore on the issue of unintended consequences and ask you this — whether in the case of Singapore, because of the way we have organised ourselves in the society that we are, is there anything special about Singapore which makes this issue of unintended consequences significant, special or problematic in any way?

David: Perhaps I can answer your question by following up on your question to Arnoud and provide a different but possibly complementary answer to what Arnoud gave about Singapore.

I am not a historian. But the way that I look at it is that in the early days of Singapore, our policymakers were functioning in survivor mode. Things were actually very bad. We had no resources. And if we did not do it properly, the outcome can be really bad. So the policymakers were responsible to make the country work, in a completely existential sense. That made them take many risks. The work of the HDB (Housing Development Board) was a complete risk. In a short time, it built hundreds and thousands of flats and apartments. If you do not build properly, a building can collapse! It was in fact a complete huge risk. It worked, and today we know HDB is one of miraculous success stories. Without the risk-taking that occurred, you would not have a port, you would not have Changi airport, and you would not have all the things that we have now. So, for many years, we were the most risk-taking government, that is, the first-generation government. Then when the second, third and fourth generation leaders come about, things were different. But it is not the leaders per se that is the issue. I think they were less risk-taking but it was because of a responsibility that they entered into. What happened was, and is, that you as a leader feel responsible that you need to make sure this place works, and you see yourself as steward of what you inherited. What happens when you see yourself as a steward? Now, if Arnoud were to hand over to me something functioning and very precious, I will be very cautious handling it because I now have a responsibility to make sure it continues to work and will do even better. I think that was a situation of unintended consequence. Sometimes, some of the problems occurred in Singapore not because people are inherently not risk-takers or that they are not competent. It was because of a good value that they have, such as a sense of responsibility and stewardship. But in a way, it could sometimes end up with a negative unintended consequence.

I will just end with a direct answer to your question about what is special or problematic about Singapore on intended consequences. I think one of our problems is that we are too networked. The same individuals are involved in so many things in Singapore, such as sitting on various boards and important committees. And what that means is that if we are all very smart and good people who do the right thing and always get it right, then Singapore is a wonderful place. And what it also means is that it takes only some of us to be incompetent, irresponsible or have bad character, and the damage could be tremendous. So the highly connected network in a small place like Singapore can be both good and bad. I think what is special about Singapore is that because of the nature of this network, the unintended consequences, positive or negative, can proceed rapidly, multiply, and magnify.

Fook Kwang: But can I follow up on that, David. Why are we so networked in this particularly way?

David: Frankly, I am not sure what the answer is, but I think part of it is historical. You have a powerful government who is very involved in every aspect of life in Singapore. You have civil servants who, even though you left the service, you would be in GLCs (government-linked companies), and then you have a public and private sector people who you co-opt and bring them together in all the various committees. So we are very networked. Often, we also end up actually believing in a common mission, which is good. But also often, because of the interpersonal relations, group dynamics and power structures, we become less likely to disagree with each other. This is human nature, and it happens too among academics. We work together, go to the same conferences, and we know each other well over time. How many times do you see an academic standing up and saying to your friend who is a fellow academic: "I think you're wrong, and your argument is flawed."

Fook Kwang: Thanks David. Let me open the floor to questions.

Audience Member #1: I have two questions, one for Arnoud and one for David, and by the way, they are excellent speeches. For Arnoud, on your indicator for how well prepared we are in the human resource sector, I may not put it at that high a level. I think that one problem we have in this rhetoric for success is that we have failed to allow for failures to be socially interpreted in a positive manner, so the cultural code is missing for interpreting failure. I believe this is a barrier for innovation, and so we are all too scared to take the alternative route. Next, for David. Your speech is so fun and it just syncs very well with all of us because, and the scary thing is, we can identify ourselves in it. What worries me is that we all tend to protect ourselves and we game the system. We look for loopholes and then try to make sure that we are able to come up on top. I think going forward, for the stability of Singapore to be able to do all the wonderful things that the future planning has in store for us, what is missing is the notion of social capital that you have alluded to. That is why I want to invite you to elaborate on this because it is so important that we do not game the system. If we can build a nation that is strong on social capital, it means that there is mutual trust and will not have these kinds of intensive network that you were talking about, but in general there is a trust across the board. And when we do see unintended consequences that are negative, then immediately we will be strong enough to step up to plug the gap and not take advantage of it.

Fook Kwang: Thank you. Arnoud, question about the failure narrative?

Arnoud: As I was looking through my slides yesterday evening, I was actually reflecting on why I had given education or the depth of human capital in Singapore such a high ranking. I think our educational system is extremely good at growing the individual. I am not sure if we are really very good at what I would call the collaborative human capital. What I mean by that is the following. When you think of Paris, many of us think about all kinds of things but one of the words that probably will come up is fashion. When you go to Paris, there is a little part of the city where you can feel what fashion is because that is where you find the designers, and the patent makers or the people who translate these crazy designs into real clothing, jewellery, perfumes and whatever. They are all there sitting together interacting with each other, learning from each other, constantly deepening their skills. If you go to Milan and you drive from Milan to Venice, you will drive along the highway where one building after another building is a medium-sized enterprise that has something to do with two big businesses, mechanical equipment and again design, the GUCCI type of that world. And you do not recognise the names but when you write down the names and later google them, you will see they all have a little part of what makes northern Italian design so strong, both in machinery and in fashion. And that is where probably the depth of our human capital is lacking. Our individuals are very well educated. But the collaborative human capital still needs to be deepened a lot more. And that is probably why, when reflecting on it yesterday evening, I was a bit optimistic when I prepared my slides.

David: Social capital is always used in a positive sense by most people. But of course, there is negative social capital and we all know it. Negative social capital is one of the good explanations for low social mobility. When people who are high in socio-economic structures actually have a lot of good social capital, you have all the connections, and you can send your kids to internship at a good company because you know the Chairman or somebody important. So those are part of social capital, and there is nothing wrong with that per se, and we want the good for our kids.

But the same situation, from a different perspective, can also be a case of negative social capital if we agree that low social mobility is a negative consequence. So it is important to distinguish between positive and negative social capital, while both may be referring to the same social networks.

But of course, the question was about building positive social capital to counter negative unintended consequences. First, I just want to clarify that I am not saying that human beings are inherently bad and we all will go and cut off the tail of the rat (in the earlier story of unintended consequences from pest control measures). What I am simply saying is that there can be perverse effects that happened and were unintended. And note that unintended consequences can be positive, and they need not always be negative. So the notion of unintended consequences does not presuppose a bad human nature with people out to gain for self and game the system.

The way I will address your question on positive social capital is this. Yes, you have to build trust in Singapore, and that was why I concluded my talk with trust building. But before you can successfully build trust, you actually have to first take the perspective of the people. A good policymaker can have the best intentions, but if you do not understand the perspective of the people whom you need to get the buy-in for a policy, then you will not be able to build the trust. I think perspective-taking is very important. As a policymaker or leader, we want you to have competence and character. But perspective-taking is the important thing that I think we need to build up for everyone in Singapore, including both people and their leaders. I always say that in Singapore, we are very good in getting our economics right, and we are actually quite good nowadays in getting our politics right, but we are not very good in getting our psychology right. I think the psychology of perspective-taking — that is the part that is lacking. And it is not all the government's fault. All of us should be involved in building trust. If I love Singapore and if I think that the government is generally made up of good individuals with good intentions, then I should and will step up when things fail, right? In fact, many of us do that, in different ways. So if some public policies or some part of a policy, such as population policies, have not worked well and are producing negative unintended consequences, then we should say, "Well, you guys in the government did not handle this well. I am going to step up now." I think that is the particular point that we can agree completely and focus on, about building trust and social capital to counter negative unintended consequences, and not necessarily having to assume we are dealing with bad people out to game the system for self.

Audience Member #2: I just have an observation that Singapore is such a high cost society and that perhaps inhibits our ability to innovate.

Arnoud: It is an interesting hypothesis and the academic in me says this is worth some research. But just looking at the face of it, most of the places that we would consider to be very innovative are actually quite expensive to live. Think about London, Paris, and Silicon Valley. And think about Finland and Helsinki. These are not cheap places to live, so I would say true innovation is not uncorrelated with high GDP and high cost of living. The second point is that I agree with you that Singapore is a place where it can be costly to live. But when I asked my students from China, they seem to get by ok with very low budget in Singapore. Maybe it is also a little bit of sacrifices one is willing to make. Where do you live and how do you live? Where do you eat and what do you do? So Singapore is not always costly, but maybe my second point is more tongue-in-cheek than anything else.

Fook Kwang: Thank you Arnoud. I think that is a good point about London and Silicon Valley, although someone told me that in Taiwan you are allowed to operate your business from your own homes, whereas I think in the case of Singapore, our HDB rules do not allow us to do that.

David: I think your (Fook Kwang) comment relates to a very relevant issue. I can understand why we need zoning policies on residential versus business use of space. Singapore is a small place, and yes, people will complain about the inconveniences that may or will occur when certain zoning policies are not in place. But a particular zoning policy can have many unintended consequences. If we cannot have residents living in a business district, then much of the area will be underused and not have the vibrancy in the evenings and weekends when everyone working there has gone back to their homes. If we cannot live at or near where we work, then we cannot get back during the lunch break to see our young children or elderly parents and take care of their needs, and then get back to work. This makes it harder to balance, manage or integrate work life and family life. So a zoning policy that is rigid and not adaptive will provide many problems and unintended consequences, even though they originated from good goals with positive intended consequences. This is related to the difficult issue of what to do with AirBnB and other online services that URA (Urban Redevelopment Authority) and MND (Ministry of National Development) have to deal with, where there is a marketplace and broker service for leasing residential homes for short-term accommodation. There appears to be a trade-off issue here. I have previously written on this, on how we can adopt a paradoxical approach and potentially turn this apparently zero-sum trade-off situation into a win-win situation integrating the goals of income generation for certain segments of the population, tourism promotion, optimisation of space use and so on.

But my main point here is that sometimes we think we were being very principled, adhering to legal rules or regulations and being very fair in our actions, but their consequences were unintended and negative. So the issue is not that policymakers are inherently risk-adverse or the cost of living in Singapore. I think the issue is about structures and processes, and the way we adhere to certain values or principles. All originated and proceeded with good intentions, but may have become at least not as adaptive to changing needs and contexts, if not maladaptive. I would not say we have gone overboard in adhering certain good values. But perhaps sometimes we forgot that there are other good and important values that we all also believe in and want to promote, and we must not neglect them in our belief and zeal to adhere to the starting values. I think different distinct values need not be mutually exclusive if we are able to adopt paradoxical thinking in policymaking. And ironically, if we don't think paradoxically and think only in terms of trade-offs, we may actually sacrifice a value that we believe in and even end up not achieving all our value-driven goals.

Fook Kwang: Can I ask you, David, to elaborate on the issue of anticipated and unanticipated unintended consequences that you mentioned earlier in your talk? As I understand your presentation, you seem to be making the point that if policymakers are upfront about the anticipated unintended consequences, then the outcomes will be different than if they keep quiet about their anticipated unintended consequences. But there are trade-offs and questions of accountability and so on. And if you want to, you can also comment on the population example that you alluded to in your talk.

David: Well, I will never know the true answer for some situations, especially I was not directly involved in the decision-making of policies. So in cases that I do not know all the facts in the policy decision-making process, I can only speculate and respond constructively and responsibly. The way I see it is this, speaking in general and putting aside for now the population issue. I think it is not true that policymakers have this anticipated negative outcome that they tried to hide it from you. I do not think it works that way in Singapore. I think what happened is that sometimes policymakers think there is no time for them to explain the issues and decision-making, or they never think about the need for explaining. Things happen and so the policymaker deal with them. But having said that, there is also a human self-serving bias in every one of us, that we tend to believe we were not the ones responsible for negative outcomes, even for some quite obvious mistakes.

Now, on the issue of public transport, the population size was increasing rapidly but our infrastructure was not catching up. I cannot believe that no one in the civil service and no politician had thought about the need to match infrastructure and population size. It is just impossible because this is about basic planning and not about an unfair criticism based on hindsight. Perhaps the structures and processes of deliberations and decision-making prevented some issues or disagreements from teaching the higher level that it should, and at the same time, there was an underestimation of the extent of the anticipated unintended consequence. I can imagine the following possible internal discussions. Some thought through and knew about the issues and anticipated the unintended consequences, but they said, "No choice, the economy needs this population increase, we need to do this and do this now, and we just do it." Then there were others who were a little more cautious and said, "Are you sure? We must think about social integration and so on". Remember this was before 2011. And so some said, "Don't worry. Singaporeans are smart and rational, and they will just go along and they will just adapt to the population increase and changes." So I think the population issue was a judgment call that was made, which is completely different from saying that the unintended consequences was unanticipated. It was anticipated, but it was underestimated.

Arnoud: Just a quick comment on that. This is more a personal comment and it has nothing to do with politics or civil service but to do with the job that I have now and in the jobs that I had before. When you are in a senior management position and you take a decision, you often know that there are anticipated unintended consequences. I think that most of us in my position would then say, "We'll deal with them when they come up." For the good of the organisation, for the good of the country, or perhaps other good reasons, we need to take this decision. We can anticipate that there are some unintended consequences, and when they arise, we will deal with them. But then it is actually quite human to then forget about them. And then they suddenly arise and you have to deal with them in a bit of a hasty way. I think that is a phenomenon that I have seen in business. I am not talking about civil service but I have seen in business that phenomenon. Yes, we anticipate consequences. We think we can deal with them when they arrive, but we forget about that because the world is complex and we have other priorities and so on. I see that happening in business quite regularly.

Fook Kwang: We have about five minutes left for this panel discussion. We can take one or two more questions. So let me turn to you Arnoud, about this question of innovation. I think you were too positive about Singapore and I do worry about the fact that we have so few very well-known world-class local Singapore companies at that leading edge of innovation. Even though there have been many national committees formed, we seem to have to struggle with producing the large world-class Singapore companies. What is the problem?

Arnoud: This is an issue that I have been thinking about a lot, especially because of my immediate environment and that is the universities. I say universities because NUS (National University of Singapore) and NTU (Nanyang Technological University) too — we are all in the same situation. I do observe a real major change over the last five to ten years, and that is there is now a real willingness by our young people, and our not-so-young alumni too, to actually take the risk to set up their own company. Like you (Fook Kwang), I have not seen many, if any, of those really growing into what is described in the literature as a unicorn, one that grows into a company with a billion-dollar turnover. I have not seen those. We always go back to the success we have in water treatment and one or two other companies that we have in marine engineering. But in most cases, one has to be realistic that it had a lot to do with the priorities of the country. It is not independent of the priorities of the country. Water was an important issue. Marine engineering is built on the long tradition that we had with the shipyards here in Singapore. So you wonder why that growth is not happening, why the young companies cannot grow to, not necessarily a unicorn, but even just a hundred or fifty million dollar company. I come back to the six dimensions in my talk. I think we really have an issue in terms of the fact that we see innovation and growing of companies as too much of a technical issue. And we do not spend enough time on what is the financial engineering needed and what is the approach to markets that we need to have. When I say approach, it is not marketing per se but how do we build up markets? How do we reach out to faraway markets, whether they are in the north of China or in Japan or in the United States or Europe? How do we build up the relationships and networks with those markets? That is what we are suffering from. As I said, the lack of financial engineering and a lack of good access to markets. So we say the market sizes here are not big enough. But then again, I ask my students, "Hey, there is a market of 250 million next door! Why don't you go there?" They look at me and said, "Well, Prof, I really don't want to go and live in

Medan", or "I don't want to live in Surabaya, and Jakarta has all these traffic jams." "Is this where I want to go and live? Singapore is so great, this is such a buzzy city to live in." So my point to conclude is that we need to look a lot more at the soft side of innovation, rather than at the hard side. I think we are very good in research and development. But we really need to think more about what is the absorptive capacity for the country for all this output that we have in research and development, and what is the soft side of innovation. There is a lot of work to be done.

Fook Kwang: Thank you, Arnoud. David, you spoke about Singapore being an adaptive learning society, that this is the next phase of development and that this is going to be very important. Can I ask you if you had to make one change in Singapore, one fundamental change whether it is public policy or whatever so that we can be a better adaptive learning society, what would it be?

David: Well, I assume we are talking about one foundational change that is practically feasible. I think we need to have a better attitude towards diversity in a way that Arnoud has explained diversity. I am thinking beyond harmony and integration among the different races. I think the problem is the diversity of ideas, and every one of us is still not very good at dealing with this, and by the way this includes academics. I think as academics, most of us are very stubborn about our ideas. When people do not agree with us, we get upset. But I think that is also true about our policymakers. And that is also true about our civil servants. Why? Because they have all spent so much time on the issues, and they are so smart, and they believe strongly in what they do. And I think that is the problem we have in dealing with the diversity of ideas. It seems to me that sometimes, the smarter you are, the less open you are to diversity of ideas. Because you have invested so much, you thought so much about the issues, and you are quite confident. And I think many of us are too concerned about being wrong, too concerned about saying or admitting that you are wrong. We need to realise that sometimes it is okay to be wrong.

Arnoud: I actually think that Singapore is pretty good at experimentation and cutting its losses. If it does not work, lets talk about it. But what you do not do is talking about the failures and say, "What do we learn from it?" An example that I have followed over the years is that, in the beginning of 2000, Singapore wanted to become a "global schoolhouse" and it was one of the reasons why I am here. I came here with INSEAD a long time ago. And then suddenly that word disappeared but nobody asked, "Why is it disappearing?", "What is happening?", "What is going wrong with it?", and "Why do we decide differently?" I am sure there were internal discussions and analyses have been made. But it is, for me, an example of not talking enough about the failures. It is an innocuous example because there were probably good reasons why it was stopped. But we are not very good at openly talking about, "Okay, we tried this out, it didn't work. Why didn't it work? What do we learn from it?" And also making these learnings public. Therefore, if I could give one advice, it is to be more open about your failures.

Fook Kwang: Thank you, Arnoud and David. Please join me in showing our appreciation to the two speakers.

Part II

Chapter 4

Singapore's Smart Nation Initiative: Can We Future-Proof Ourselves?

Tan Kok Yam

I am glad and honoured to be here. I am really looking forward to a frank and open discussion after my presentation. I want to begin with the sentiments that I believe many of us as individuals, a society, a company or a country, have on smart nation and this whole idea of smartness and digital revolution. A few of us are cynical that it is mostly hype. A few of us are fearful of what it would do to us, our livelihood, how we live, and so on. But I think the majority of us are just a little bewildered, a little conscious that these things will affect how we do things in a massive way, but just not sure how it affects us individually and specifically. Therefore, I will keep my presentation very broad and open for the purpose of soliciting your views and having a meaningful discussion later.

I will start by stating the obvious, and then talk about the two ways we think about smartness — the application of smartness in a city or a country and the concept of liveability and livelihood. I will end with a "so what?" question, and that is, "What do we do given what we know about how it will affect liveability and livelihood?"

Let me state the obvious. It will happen to us — technology disruptions will hit us at an alarming and disruptive pace, whatever we do or do not do. Our children are going to be addicted to the smartphone, regardless of whether there is a smart nation or not. Pokémon Go will come and go regardless of whatever we do. We will be affected by what is happening outside, in terms of the use of Facebook, WhatsApp, Google, use of the internet, cyber-hacking, and so on. We will all be affected by these external factors and that is independent of what we do and how we respond as an individual or as a society.

Why are we so sure that it will happen? The reason is not because of science. It is because of economics. The sheer price of computing today is so low that you are able to have pretty high compute power available just in your smartphone. In addition, sensors are so cheap that you can do anything with it. So, with the falling price of computing, you have connectivity. Information is connected, and I can search for anything right now, from cute kittens to online data about anybody. Things can now be connected because the sensors are so cheap that there can be a sensor on the chair or a sensor on the stage. With all this connectivity, we get new ways of doing things, new ways to interact, new business models, new ways to gather information. When we have these digitised ways of doing things, we collect a lot of data. When we pay cash, there is no record of debt. Imagine paying digitally by PAYLAH, or credit card and so on, there is now a digital trail of that particular payment. You add all that up, and we have a tsunami of data. What is more, we have the computation power to deal with the data. So data itself becomes an asset and when data is an asset, it feeds the new social and business models. WhatsApp is free because you are paying for it by the data that you contribute and that fuels additional businesses and opportunities. Therefore, falling cost of computing, increased digital connectivity, and rising computational power lead to greater opportunities as well as uncertainty, which will affect our liveability and livelihood.

There are two aspects of liveability. The first aspect is what I would call the visible smart. The application that you have to download is visible. The lamppost that you see with sensors and cameras on it is visible. You have some smart home devices, and that is visible too. The issue about visible smart is that it has to be human-centric in nature because the technology has to interact with the individual. It cannot be an application that nobody wants to use. It cannot be a sensor or CCTV camera that people are fearful of, and end up not make people feel more secure but make people fear being seen by the CCTV.

There is an invisible smart as well. An overhead bridge is brick-and-mortar, but where we place an overhead bridge can be informed by the data that we collect. This could be the geospatial information that we collect which gives us the knowledge of the flow of people going across the road and the demographics of the people. So, we will know where the overhead bridge is necessary, and where do we need to have an overhead bridge that has a lift to help the elderly go up the bridge. Buses are also brick-and-mortar but we know when a bus is overcrowded or delayed from the information on bus flow that we collect from sensors. We can then regulate by either injecting more buses or ask the transport provider to do something about their route over time. So this is something that is already happening — it is brick-and-mortar but it is an example of the invisible smart. Healthcare is yet another example. If we know the pattern of which elderly comes back more often than others after discharged from the hospital, we may be able to detect a certain way that we can improve the manner of treatment so that there are less of these return cases and we improve healthcare options. This again is premised on the smart use of data. A final example is the lift. If we know when the lift is going to break down before it does because we have collected all the machine data about it, then we can make lifts that are much more reliable.

In all these machine intelligence, the decisions are made by data analytics. Data science is moving very fast and there is increasing autonomy in terms of how machines are deciding on these things, whether it is a simple machine learning that you can download from website or a deep learning algorithm. But when we use machine learning and AI more to make judgments such as to decide where to place resources and how to recruit people, the opportunities and the potential are tremendous. So it is important that we can deal with the various ethics issues by rationally discussing them, not out of fear, but with the knowledge of what or where are the bounds that we should set the software. This is, I think, a very important question that all of us will have to grapple with, with the increasing use of machine intelligence.

Let me now discuss the aspect of livelihood. We know that jobs always come and go. The issue we face now is not that jobs will change with technology but the rate of change. In the past, it may take one generation, or half a generation at least, to have fundamental change in the workplace, to have to refresh your own set of skills, and so on. Now, the change could be in three or five years. The set of skills that are marketable will also change over time. So the workforce will have to cope with the faster rate of change in terms of the kind of jobs available and keep ourselves updated and upgraded. But it is not only the level and depth of technical skills that we require, but also the ability to integrate the problem statements to technical solutions.

Let me now talk a little about data because it seems remiss of me not to talk about data in a presentation on smart nation. Data is actually not the new oil — it is much more than that. If I give you a barrel of oil, I no longer have that barrel of oil. But if I give you a piece of data, I still have that piece of data. It is a multiplicative effect, and the economy of data is different from the economy of oil.

There are three areas that countries or societies have to grapple with when using data. These are (1) privacy versus use, (2) private versus public, and (3) new concepts of trust. The key questions in the area of privacy versus use are how to manage the need for data privacy and the heterogeneous effect that data sharing has on different people, and how can we maximally use data for the good of society. In the area of private versus public, the key question is how can we incentivise data owners so that we extract more value from the data for the benefit of the economy and society. Finally, we will need to deal with new concepts of trust. For example, with the digitisation of our lives, trust may be measured in new ways and need not be based on personal interactions. For example, a company in China has given credit scores to different users of their platform. If you have a high credit score, you can go to a hotel and need not leave your credit card at the lobby. Credit scores derived from personal data become a new way to measure trust.

Let me conclude with how a smart nation can be a nation where people can chase their dreams and live meaningful and fulfilled lives. It will require three things.

First, it is important to have openness of platforms, where there is open sharing of information, data, knowledge, software and open source ideas so that all these can be integrated to solve issues that society may have. So, for a start, we must learn to deal with the openness of platforms.

The second point is the idea about the "internet of hands". This refers to using the internet not only just to raise voices and opinions, but as a tool for society to help one another and to do public service. It could be using an application to report to the authorities a clogged drain or some malfunctioning public amenities that need to be fixed or calling for medical help in an emergency. It is about democratising the provision of public service.

The final point is about the meeting of minds. We need to encourage people from different disciplines and people with different perspectives to come together to create meaningful solutions that have application to the market, people, users and society.

So, there are three important points for Singapore to be a smart nation — (1) openness of platforms; (2) internet of hands; and (3) meeting of minds. We need to come together to work on them, for technology to enable people to chase their dreams and live meaningful and fulfilling lives.

Thank you very much.

Chapter 5

Dealing with Uncertainty: Comparing Public and Private Sector Organisations in Singapore

Neo Boon Siong

I will share with you some observations I have from working with both the public and private sectors in recent years and my views on the approaches they take to deal with uncertainty. I define uncertainty as the lack of reliable or accurate information to predict the future and prepare adequately for emerging developments. Uncertainty leads to a fear of what is coming, especially given the tremendous ongoing changes and disruptions to jobs, the economy and our society. The problem of uncertainty is not just that we do not fully understand the consequences but also the lack of ability to adequately prepare for what is coming. Uncertainty is caused by increasing complexity of the issues that we are dealing with, and the unexpected consequences, which may not turn out the way that we had figured out, although not necessarily unanticipated as David mentioned earlier in his presentation. Uncertainty is also caused by the rapid rate of change. When complexity and change are combined, the degree of uncertainty is heightened.

When I compare the private and public sectors in Singapore, I find that their responses to uncertainty are actually a lot more similar than different. Let me begin with the common responses to uncertainty. You will probably find these responses familiar. These include ignoring, denying, doing more of the same, and overreacting out of fear. When faced with uncertainty, the initial response is almost always to ignore it; and then when it actually begins to surface, we deny it because it does not fit the patterns of what we have experienced and learned; and when we are under pressure, we actually do more of the same; and then when something goes wrong, we over-react out of fear.

The CFE (Committee on the Future Economy) released its report last week. But if you go back to read the 2011 Economic Strategies Committee's report, there was a lot of focus on productivity. We still struggle with productivity after six years. We continue to say that while that is a long term thing that we cannot expect too immediate results.

If you examine it, you will see that our response actually fits this pattern — we ignore it, we deny it, we actually do more of the same. Our typical response to productivity improvements is to train the workers. Worker training is our number one approach. But today, the problem with productivity in Singapore institutions and organisations is not the worker — it is the managers and the leaders. The workers are trained with knowledge and skills that they cannot use because they come back to an organisation system that has been designed not to use the knowledge and skills that they have been trained to do. But we do not know how to deal with the managers and the leaders of an organisation when the major cause of productivity is not worker skill but managerial mindset, the business model, and the organisational system. Yet, we continue to do the same thing and we expect different results.

When I look at the private sector, it is no different. The biggest threats facing banks today are Fintech. Again, the initial response of banks is to ignore it or deny it. Why ignore it? Because the Fintech startups are targeting customers that we actually are not interested in. Unserved or underserved customers, low profit customers, and unprofitable customers that we do not really care about. When Fintech began to gain traction, we deny that it would ever break into our territory, and then when it became more of a threat, we hunker down and push more of our current products and services to the same group of markets and customers.

But uncertainty need not undermine our ongoing success. It is really how we respond that matters. Success or failure is dependent on how an organisation responds to opportunities and challenges. That is where the problem comes in. First, our current established structures hamper our ability to respond in a strategic manner. The current resources and skills that we have today in our organisations — both private and public — are honed to compete in the current product market space and deal with the current problems, and not really for adapting to undefined areas. To respond to something so uncertain will be considered a waste of investment and it will not pass their ROI (return of investment) and finance. Second, our current systems and structures are configured to achieve standardisation and economies of scale, and not for creative responses to evolving situations. Our organisational templates are the problems. Third, our control processes and practices are designed to ensure consistency and reduce errors, and not for speed and for flexibility.

How did our assets become liabilities? First, because once we invest in assets, we want to continue to milk them for as long as possible rather than invest in new ones. Our legacy IT (information technology) systems is a constraint and not a facilitator of innovation. Similarly, you put a new proposal to a current expert that you employ within an organisation. The experts will evaluate the new proposal based on their current understanding and knowledge and tell you all the risks and problems of what your new proposal will have rather than the new possibilities. Finally, the established ecosystem is also a problem — your partners and distributors want something that works and does not have a high risk of failure.

Our assumptions also limit our strategic response. We always assume that because we have been successful, and we have the track record and experience, the industry understanding and the resources, and therefore we can outlast anyone. But consider Singapore as a whole and look at the approach that we have taken because of our success. Unfortunately, if you look at the last few years, we have spent more money in more areas with less results than we had earlier. Simply because we have the money. Also, our regulations are often designed to protect the current players rather than to allow new players to come in. Because regulation, by design, is for current activities, it cannot regulate something that is not yet there.

Our past success creates strategic blind spots. What is successful cannot be challenged. They will point out to you this is what has happened in the last 40 years and it has worked for us. Whether it be our traditional definition of meritocracy or our traditional way of school admission, it is difficult to challenge. Our operational efficiency actually makes us focus on current problems rather than new areas. We often evaluate the new technologies with current activities in mind rather than with what is coming. We are more concerned with operational risks and therefore we rather stick with tried-and-tested programmes rather than take on something that we do not know. There lies our problem. Singapore's success, built on an efficient rule-based system, has the unintended or unintentional consequences of diminishing our capacity to deal with an uncertain and disruptive environment. This is a case where I am not sure we had anticipated the unintended consequence.

Let me use the challenges that we have in our whole-of-government collaboration as an example. We have been very effective as a civil service because of the unique approach that we have taken called a statutory board. Very cleverly, with some autonomy in finance and human resources, a very clear focused mission and high quality people who are not distracted and clear KPIs (key performance indicators), we have achieved enormous results through statutory boards. HDB (Housing Development Board) was an early example. Another example is EDB (Economic Development Board) that created jobs. So that has become a de facto response. Every time we have a problem, we create a new statutory board. I think we have created more new statutory boards in the last few years than we did the previous 40 years. But when problems become more complex and no longer fall neatly into a functional role that a typical statutory board has, and yet you begin to define the problem within the boundaries of your own role and mission, and because your KPIs are so clear cut, working with other agencies is actually a very inefficient way for you to deal with it. We talk about the "One Service Application". When the MSO (Municipal Services Office) was created, I was very embarrassed as a Singaporean. That is a clearest sign of how our agencies cannot work together to solve simple municipal problems. To have to create something like this is an embarrassment to us. Even worse, the Prime Minister had to speak on the same subject at two National Day Rallies in a row. But that is the outcome of a very efficient modular silo system that we have created to solve very simple, straightforward and understandable problems that we had.

The comparisons between private and public are less significant. I will compare them in terms of time frame, strategy, execution, and challenges.

On the issue of time frame, the private sector tends to be more short term focused. The strategy for private sector tends to be one of cutting cost and being opportunistic. I was on the board of OCBC during the last financial crisis, and the Bank acquired the ING private bank that today is the Bank of Singapore. It was an opportunistic acquisition when the European banks were pulling back. The advantage in execution in the private sector is that it can act fast, and private sector organisations adjust very quickly. What is less clear is the challenge of private sector responses to uncertainty — is it really agility or is it just ad hoc preference of a group of senior managers? Sometimes, in trying to survive, you may miss the significant innovations.

The public sector, on the other hand, tends to take a longer term perspective, which I think is good. The typical strategy is to focus on reviewing plans. They will form committees to chart future directions. The Committee on the Future Economy is just one example. The public sector is very systematic. The challenge is that it is slow, overly careful and often the strategies put forth look like very incremental changes rather than significant steps forward. When the changes to the PSLE (Primary School Leaving Examination) were announced, I wondered why changing from T-scores to a grade would need six years before implementation. At the university, we could do it in one semester. The public sector tends to be overly careful and, as a result, sometimes the response becomes too slow.

I will conclude by highlighting the need for building capacity for managing uncertainty. There are three areas. First, for both private and public sectors, we need to go beyond just focusing on efficiency to focus on exploratory innovations, which have significant built-in uncertainty. So what the MAS (Monetary Authority of Singapore) is doing in terms of its response to Fintech is quite encouraging. They created a regulatory sandbox, which basically said to Fintech players that, within a specific area, we do not need to regulate you even though you are in areas and activities that we normally regulate. But we want to watch you and learn from you, and when we begin to understand more, then we will decide how best to regulate you. That is quite a different approach to regulation that I have seen in many parts of the government. I think it is the acceptance and acknowledgement that the paths going forward are not and cannot be based on our past experience, and no matter how experienced we are, it is not going to be adequate because we are charting paths that are not taken before and are relatively unknown. That requires us to be willing to build a portfolio of activities.

Second, we need to go beyond just planning to focus on strategy agility. A typical approach of the public sector is that when something goes wrong, it will say "Let's plan". But you cannot plan on something that you do not know. If you do not have knowledge and you have no information and skills, you cannot plan. You have to start doing it and then adjust as you go, and after a while, you know how things work, and then you can plan. But today, the most fundamental philosophy within the public sector when you want to do something is to develop a masterplan. But a masterplan can only be developed in things that you know, which means that they cannot be done in areas of high uncertainty. What we need is the ability to act first and dare to act fast. So you can see why we have so many problems. Our ROI (return of investment) and our financial parameters for evaluating investments will not work. We have a problem of over-reliance on plans. We want to know the results three to five years down the road when we do not even know how it is going to work in the next three to five months. And until we know the results three to five years down the road, we would not approve it.

Finally, we need to go beyond just focusing on our current core competence in doing what we are doing, to be able to develop what we call dynamic capabilities. By that I mean the capability to reinvent our current capability. In the earlier work that I have done and explained in my book on Dynamic Governance, I looked at three sets of dynamic capabilities. I think that while Singapore is very good at continuing to think ahead and identify some of the problems that may come along, we are losing our capacity to think again what is successful and what has worked, and to challenge them before a crisis forces us to do so. We have a long way to go in developing our ability to think across boundaries, to collaborate and to innovate.

Thank you very much.

Chapter 6

Panel Discussion 2

Panelists: Tan Kok Yam, Neo Boon Siong
Moderator: Lim Lai Cheng

Lai Cheng: In this session, Kok Yam spoke about technology, intelligent systems, smart nation, and they are all very exciting. I think the question that we have, or we should be thinking about, is what is the role of government and what is the nature of public policy in this brave new world where we are all expecting digital disruption or transformation in every sector of our economy. Boon Siong provided us a conceptual framework but he did actually touch on those uncomfortable questions that we should be asking. What is the managerial mindset we should have? How should we organise the system and how should the government enable a lot more exploration, a lot more agility in the way we strategise and also developing those dynamic capabilities. So I think the two talks connected in a way and I am sure all of you in the audience have questions and comments that you would like to share.

Audience Member #1: My question is for Boon Siong. In your book "Dynamic Governance", you looked at the Singapore Civil Service. I noticed that today, you gave a very bracing assessment of the public sector and private sector organisations, which is about a failure in management, if I could put it bluntly. But in your book, you actually highlighted the strength of the public service in terms of their ability to think ahead, think across domains and to think again. I remember from reading that book that your assessment then was that the public sector in Singapore is actually well positioned to cope with an uncertain world. So I was a little surprised this morning to hear you say that the system we have developed is one that is very good for creating rules and maintaining rules but that it might have the unintended consequence of preventing us from engaging with an uncertain environment. Could you tell us more about why you have now come to this position?

Boon Siong: It is really the observations that I have as I interact and work with different organisations in the last few years. I think the system we have is still excellent and I am very proud of what we have and especially when I speak to foreign audiences about the strengths that we have in terms of making sure that the system works. We still have efficient delivery of services. My concern is really about the future. The theme for the CFE (Committee on the Future Economy) report is Pioneering for a New Generation. When I saw that, I thought it was very interesting. I wondered whether the committee thought we may have lost that. I think it is something that we need to re-ignite in order to not only survive and but to succeed. I do not think the system is broken, but I am concerned about the direction that it is going, in terms of dealing with new challenges.

Audience Member #2: I have a more specific question about the displacement effects of automation. If Uber decides to roll out autonomous vehicles, many taxi drivers could be out of work. So I am curious what you think government and private sector could work together to do to mitigate some of these consequences.

Lai Cheng: It is a very good question because it does parallel the question about the unintended consequences which might have been anticipated. I am sure the government would have anticipated some of these displacement effects of automation. So let us hear from Kok Yam.

Kok Yam: I think the thing we can do right now is to make sure that we create the space — , what you call the sandbox — to be able to have this autonomous vehicle technology tried out. So we take an approach of let's try this out and let's make sure it is safe. We want to try this out so that we can evolve and very agilely develop the rules including the traffic rules and the legislation to allow for autonomous vehicles to happen. Because if we are able to do some of these technological advances and incorporate them into our public transportation, the impact on liveability is tremendous. You can imagine a dynamic response public transport that is everywhere, ubiquitous. But the way that we are going to manage the change, whether it is in terms of legislation and changing the rules or in terms of looking at people whose jobs may be replaced and so on, is something that we have to start now and seed these ideas in place. This is so that as we go forward people can adjust, companies can adjust, governments and the rules can adjust, so that when the time comes that the technology is mature, we are in a good position to make use of it and not have to end up with a sudden disruption in terms of jobs and so on.

Lai Cheng: With technology like autonomous vehicles, we do not need all the in-betweens and many people may lose their jobs. How ready or how quickly can we adjust economically to such a situation? Has the Government thought through this?

Kok Yam: It is a global problem. I think the best way for us to adjust is to be as aware of it as possible as individuals, as education institutes, as a workforce and in our profession. And in our Singapore context, to be able to adjust and imbibe the relevant skills as far as possible and change the structure of how we work to incorporate the digital innovation. That is the best we can do. In a way it is a contest. It is something that everyone faces and if we can position ourselves well vis-à-vis the rest of the world, we can be hopeful that we still have a vibrant economy and there are still jobs and so on.

Audience Member #3: There is always this trade-off that has to be made on what extent to regulate or not regulate. We are very risk averse and intolerant of failure. We want to remove regulations but what happens when accidents, like a building collapsing, happen because of the lack of regulations? So there is this tension that will always be there on whether or not as a society we can tolerate some of these risks that come with less regulations.

Boon Siong: I think we need to be clear about the different types of risks. Those that are catastrophic, we probably do not want to take chances — we cannot afford the risk of a building falling down. But there are many other types of risk which are relatively minor. I was very concerned that, in recent years, many small procurement lapses have made big news. The impact of those lapses are relatively small but by highlighting it so much will make people super careful and super conservative. We underestimate the costs of delay. We take away from the total cost things that cannot be quantified (such as delays to projects) to achieve a small amount of quantifiable purchase of procurement price differences. We took a totally warped approach to it. So I think we need to be very clear. I do not think we can take the risk of a building collapsing, but when we only focus on the costs that can be quantified and ignore unquantifiable costs which are real, then we have a problem.

Lai Cheng: Thanks Boon Siong. Kok Yam?

Kok Yam: I think that is a very useful comment that you have made and actually the whole point is that when you look at regulation or deregulation, you cannot broad brush the thing. There is that one regulation that is so painful to everybody and there is that one thousand lines that nobody actually reads. What I think is generally true is that as a system or as individual agencies, we can do a better job of internalising the cost of regulation. So we have a problem, it could be a one percent problem but we regulate for the one hundred percent. And it may be a well thought-out regulation but we do not internalise the cost when we think about it and I think that is something we can do a little bit better. But I think in other aspects, sometimes you may need to have more rules to ensure a certain level of standardisation and interoperability, especially in the digital world. And so it is not so clear that deregulation is the best thing. But if you have a clear view in your mind of what you want to regulate, what is the platform that you want to regulate and where you should free up regulation for people to innovate and do all kinds of things, then that is where you have good regulation.

Lai Cheng: Let me just ask a question which follows from the idea of the anticipated consequences of a digital world. Kok Yam, would you say that there will be a digital divide in a smart nation between those who are digitally literate and those who are not. And do you think there will be an increasing risk of cybersecurity and how do we mitigate the increasing cyber security threats and the vulnerabilities that individuals as well as corporations have with regard to online networks. What is the government anticipating, and what are we doing to mitigate these risks?

Kok Yam: The second question is challenging but the answer is easy — the answer is yes, cybersecurity is a key issue and something that we have to think about. But we need to think about it not in a very risk averse kind of way like, "We will be hacked, so we don't do this.", or "We know this is a risk, so I don't digitise it." We have to think about it in terms of what capabilities we have to respond, how we can better react as individuals, as companies, as government, to these potential threats. Cybersecurity threat is something that happens every day; it is not something that is conceptual. Everyday people get hacked, everyday companies get hacked, and everyday governments get attacked. So it is something that we have to really be on our toes and use it as an enabler to allow us to do all the wonderful smart and digital things we want to do.

The first question is on digital divide and I will just give my personal view. I think globally there will be a digital divide but it is my hope that in Singapore, because of how our schools, how our education system is setup and so on, we can have as little of that as possible. And to look for digital divide, Singapore should be the last place to find because of the access to education, to fibre, to communication and so on. This is my short answer.

Audience Member #4: My first question is for Kok Yam. In order to inform the smart nation trajectory, you collect massive data and you look for trends. My question would be how would you address the concerns that those who are marginalised will then be further rendered invisible, including their needs. When we look at surveys and data, it is always about most Singaporeans and what their needs are. So what about the minority? What about the displaced? The second question is for Boon Siong. You were fairly critical of government response and I appreciate that. But I do think that the underlying problem here is how to manage uncertainties, and one of the outcomes of dealing with so much uncertainty is the further alienation of the ordinary man on the street. So no matter how fast moving your policies are, unless you can bring the last Singaporean with you, we would never make it. So how do we take care of that?

Kok Yam: Intuitively, I would argue to the contrary to your first question. In fact, because I am able to have datasets and I am able to have the tools to be able to slice the population, to look at anomalous patterns, look at different ways of expressing the issue from the set of data, I should be more able to pick up minority cases. It is just like in the financial world where being able to have a lot of could help a bank to detect anomalous transactions, frauds and so on. We are not looking for frauds here but the tools and the science allow us to pick out those very minority cases that may require more attention or more help in some way. But these are tools, you can use it anyway you want. It is about the intent and how you want to apply it, so I hope that sort of answers your question somewhat.

Audience Member #4: But my worry always is with the displaced individuals. Because they are already marginalised, people who do not even have an address for you to survey them. So we become so reliant on the information that we have and we use them to plan the city, and then we further marginalise those who are already left behind and soon they will be rendered invisible. So that is a worry that I think we should be cognizant of.

Boon Siong: I think the issues are actually related. The typical approach that we have is to announce big programmes on the podium to try to address certain issues, which we have been very good at. But today's problems are so complex that programmes alone, which is functional in nature usually within a particular Ministry or Statutory Board, can only be a partial approach to it. If you look at the lower income or marginalised groups, a better approach may be to look at it on a family-by-family basis because their needs cut across a whole range of areas that require a whole-of-government approach. That requires several agencies to work together and we are very reluctant to go there. But we cannot address those marginalised group problems that you talked about with programmes anymore because programmes often make certain things better but also make certain things worse. And each programme comes under a certain agency which is only concerned about achieving the KPIs (key performance indicators) of the programme, almost to the exclusion of impact on other areas. So why don't we take a different approach? I think it is our policy mindset that limits our approach to those solutions. So it is similar, you get all kinds of data but different agencies will look at the data within the mindset and the assumptions that they have given the mission and the role that they perform. So the data does not change the way we approach problems, it reinforced the way the mindset that we have.

Lai Cheng: I am positive that in this hybrid reality, it is technology that will enhance our ability to reach out rather than to further divide. Do you want to add on, Kok Yam?

Kok Yam: I agree that when we collect data we have to be very careful about the biases so that for those parts that we do not collect; we do not inadvertently ignore them because we are unable to collect. However, I do intuitively feel that the more you are able to collect the information and the more sources of truth that you have on the condition of the individual or the household, then the more you are able to sieve out problems and to apply the correct help. So that is my broad answer.

Audience Member #5: I want to come back to the idea of data sharing and the opportunities that come from data. The unintended consequence of the PDPA (Privacy and Data Protection Act) is that it may create more silos and vulcanised our data such as it starts to stymie the potential of this data. So could we go to a situation where we craft data as a public good, and have some anonymised data that we can all pool, share and access the information for our collective good.

Lai Cheng: I will ask Kok Yam to answer this question on data and whether we can make data a free commodity that everyone can share.

Kok Yam: On the public sector side, we are taking steps to do so. Where we can release the data as open data, we release it out. We tried to do it in machine-friendly and machine-readable mode. We try to have meaningful datasets and we are seeing some results of people being able to use that and to create value out of the data. But you asked a broader question, which is about how all of us individuals regard our data. Is it a public good or does it belong to me? Today, the general philosophy is that my data, any piece of data that is attributable to me belongs to me. That is generally the Western way of looking at it, and we sort of adopted that as a reference. I agree we need to have that discussion but it is not something that the Government can unilaterally say from now on all your data belongs to everybody. Also it cannot work this way, and it has to be a process of being able to have those conversations, which I think is valuable. The points you raised are valuable, and we need to be able to be more open about this. If we can share more health data, imagine the impact and the impact on drug discovery, on being able to have better treatments and so on. So the value is tremendous and it is worthwhile to have those conversations.

Lai Cheng: Last question is for Boon Siong. As the Dean, share with us what is Nanyang Business School at NTU (Nanyang Technological University) doing differently to prepare better our younger Singaporeans.

Boon Siong: This is my second round as Dean. When I was asked to be Dean again last year, I was in fact very concerned with some of the developments that Kok Yam presented and the impact on professional jobs for our students. All our jobs are at stake. Employers told me that in three to five years they would probably hire less than half of the number of students they were taking from us today. All the jobs that our entry-level professionals go into can be done by sophisticated AI-enabled machines, whether it be bankers or auditors or marketing professionals or credit analysts. So the way we prepare our people for the jobs of the future cannot be the same as we are doing it today. Today, we are preparing them for jobs that exist today. We do not know how to prepare them for the jobs that do not yet exist. So we have exactly the same problem that I spoke about that relates to both the public and the private sector. So the approach I have taken was to set up a task force. I told them to go deep and go explore the issues. We looked at a number of universities and how they have approached it. We think the responses are very superficial and not adequate.

I think ultimately it is about how people learn. Assuming that a graduate will now deal with a very sophisticated machine that do most of the work. It is just like a pilot being trained to fly a plane but when you go on a flight, they do not fly the plane. They monitor a machine and they need to know how to, what to do if some of those instruments give them data or feedback that are not in line within a control parameters. Many of us learn to make those judgements through many years of experience. The challenge is that our new graduates of the future will have to do that without having to do the work themselves because no company will hire them to do the work when the machine can do it more efficiently at a fraction of the cost. So how do you develop that judgment, learn to make decisions, learn to assess exceptions, learn to know whether this is an exception thrown up by the machine is really high-risk or routine. For that to happen, you need to know the context of how the data come about. Data without context is meaningless. Today, the machine is still limited and for the foreseeable future, it will still be limited by the ability to understand the context. That is where the human can incorporate value, context and professional technical competence, and we can do that in the training that enables our people to continue to learn without having to do the work themselves from day one.

Lai Cheng: Thank you Boon Siong. Ladies and gentlemen, a round of applause for our two speakers and thank you for your participation.

Part III

Chapter 7

Unexpected Outcomes of Healthcare in Singapore

Jeremy Lim

I will briefly cover a few topics on healthcare in Singapore and some of its unintended outcomes so that we have more time for discussion later. Please take the typology or the nomenclature for unintended consequences that David used earlier in his presentation to guide some of the thinking here.

Let me first state that, at its core and highest level, the objectives of a healthcare system are very simple. All healthcare planners aspire to achieve a high quality, affordable and universally accessible healthcare system. That is very straightforward; the challenge is balancing these often conflicting or competing ambitions. Imagine quality, cost and access as the three corners of a triangle. Geometry dictates that as two of these corners move closer together, they necessarily move further away from the third corner, thus elegantly depicting the difficult choices and trade-offs that we have to make in healthcare. How the emphasis placed on quality, cost and access differs across different countries and how these emphases change over time as societies evolve collectively make health policies very dynamic. There are hence stark differences in how healthcare services are designed and delivered in different societies. At its core, the issues are very straightforward, but unintended consequences come about because we try to target some of these issues without a greater appreciation of the magnitude of the impact on the other aspects related to costs, quality, and access.

There are many factors that can affect an individual's health. Health is a complex adaptive system because the determinants of health are multiple, complex and interelated. A single health issue like obesity would have multiple causal and inter-relating loops, making myriad consequences of a single policy intervention inevitable. The complexity, inter-relations and externalities that drive unintended consequences are quite beyond complete human understanding. Suffice to say that therefore we should approach health as a complex adaptive system, recognising that all we have are theories and we need to figure out how to move forward with our limited understanding. We are also living in a VUCA (volatile, uncertain, complex, ambiguous) world and this is especially so in health with both a longevity dividend and epidemics of chronic diseases. These are unprecedented times with no good models to learn from. This necessitates lots of humility and a healthy dose of what Deng Xiaoping described as "crossing the river by feeling the stones".

Intellectually, it is not difficult to recognise that health is a complex adaptive system. But emotionally and politically, we want to feel that we are in control, and "quick fixes" and "magic bullets" become attractive. One of the examples that we commonly talked about revolves around bed crunch. It is very common to have letters in the newspaper complaining about waiting time. So the quick fix is to add more hospitals and more beds, and have healthcare workers work even harder. But the solution to the bed crunch is not flogging the workhorses of the Singapore healthcare system even harder. In systems thinking nomenclature, this would merely be a "symptomatic solution" akin to aspirin for a headache. The "fundamental solution" lies in augmenting the rest of the healthcare system. That is why we now talk about integrated clusters that include primary care, the acute hospitals, long-term care, community hospitals, and so on. Systems thinking has really come into its play in the Singapore healthcare system.

Ideal policy makers are those who have been hit, and have the strength to pick themselves up, the tenacity to keep moving ahead, and the humility to learn. The ideal policy making stance would be thus less about getting it right but not getting it irreversibly wrong, and having the "system flex" to course correct. I will just discuss two examples in the Singapore context. The first is on health insurance and managed care, and the second is on medical manpower planning.

First, let us look at health insurance and managed care. The context is that many doctors were unhappy that TPAs (Third Party Administrators) were charging them fees for referring patients to them. Now, this has been a long-standing practice which has been going on for the last thirty or forty years. But last year the government, through the Singapore Medical Council, decided to intervene. The point being was that it had decided that these TPAs were charging too much. It was not what was reasonable. This amount, in the form of a percentage of the medical fee, can be quite a lot of money as the TPAs move into the specialists' space. The Singapore Medical Council thus issued guidance declaring that paying agents a percentage of the medical fees was unlawful. The intervention was not placed with the TPAs because they are unregulated entities, forcing the Singapore Medical Council to adopt as the point of leverage individual doctors. We doctors received guidance that doctors should not be entering into agreements with managed care companies where the referral fee is a percentage of total fees, and doing so would be a breach of the ethical code and subjecting us to potential disciplinary action.

Here, I think we did not do so well. First, the Singapore Medical Council did not consult the doctors and the managed care providers. The first time most of us knew about this was reading about it in the newspapers. Second, where we also did not do very well was in trying to understand why this has happened. The intervention has suddenly thrown the market into complete disarray, with huge costs potentially imposed on the doctors and the managed care providers. We should have asked why if TPAs are not performing a societally useful function, have been around for the last thirty years, and why insurers, employers and doctors were willing to pay these entities. Note that this is a voluntary arrangement — no one is forcing the doctors to enter into any of these arrangements. I think that what we have done is an example of a rather imprudent policymaking where the unintended consequences are still being played out. Some managed care providers will just change the formula of how they bill doctors, by just removing the percentage sign but nothing else will change. Some doctors will withdraw from managed care schemes and suffer reduced patient volumes, whilst patients also suffer from the limiting of care options and even worse, having to switch away from a long-standing care provider. I think in this instance, it is worthwhile to go back to first principles, map out the entire ecosystem and ask what are the roles and responsibilities of each of these players and how can the government intervene much more strategically from a policy point of view to make sure that the system continues to function well.

Related to the role of the TPAs is the guideline on fees. I think fee setting has become a massive issue in the milieu of too many doctors in certain specialties and no constraints on pricing. When we have too many doctors, the unit profit from each procedure has to go up to ensure everyone ending up with the same income. When I was a surgeon in training in the public hospital, we were doing gastroscopies (endoscopic inspection of the stomach) and patients were charged a fee of a few hundred dollars. I remember the fee to the doctors was about $50 for each case that we did. Fast forward two decades and some private specialists are charging seven to ten thousand dollars as the doctors' fee for the same procedure.

In the scenario where we have a surfeit of doctors and relatively reduction of patient volumes per doctor, doctors' incomes would ironically not precipitously decline. Instead doctors would figure out how much we want to earn and then work backwards to see how much we want to charge patients. And because most of us are on indemnity plans, meaning that our insurer or our employer will essentially pay what the doctors ask for, doctors have been much less restrained. Previously we had a guideline on fees that was deemed to be anti-competitive. The Singapore Medical Association challenged this. It sought legal opinion, decided that it was not worth the challenge, withdrew it and guidelines on how to price were removed.

The second example is medical manpower planning. This is one aspect of our healthcare policy making that is remarkable in how consistently wrong we have been. Over the last thirty or forty years, so many policies have been reversed because there have been unintended consequences, and because we have not thought through. Medical manpower planning in Singapore has been fraught with U-turns and policy unwinding, and the current reforms will be no different.

When I was in medical school, there were initially almost two hundred foreign medical schools that were recognised. And then the authorities embraced an economic theory of supplier-induced demand, meaning that we as doctors would generate our own supply. Therefore, the solution was to restrict the number of doctors. So, 200 recognised foreign medical schools shrunk down to just 10 schools. Then, as the enormity of ageing or the longevity dividend was recognised and more fully appreciated, the government made this massive U-turn and said we do not have enough doctors. So instead of one local medical school, let us have two medical schools, and later even three! When I was in medical school, there were less than

150 of us in a cohort. Today, there are 500 medical students graduating.

Moreover, within certain specialties, we have doctors who do not have jobs. For those of you who are in the public healthcare system, you would be aware that in certain specialties such as ENT (Ear, Nose, Throat) and ophthalmology, the junior doctors upon completing training are essentially being told that "You don't have a job, please go somewhere where you have a job." I think that is how a market should work but this is a market where we are producing specialists at very high cost to the taxpayer. So rather than let the market work things out after they have exited as specialists, we should be a little more proactive and figure out the numbers earlier.

The irony is that, nationally, we are still probably a little short of doctors in some specialties. We are very short of primary care physicians, palliative care physicians and geriatricians. But we probably have too many obstetrician, ophthalmologist, plastic surgeons, and dermatologists. I suspect the thinking had been that if doctors do not have jobs, they will just flow into areas where they have jobs. But some of the unintended consequences or outcomes are that doctors start to flow outside Singapore because the world is short globally of 12.5 million healthcare professionals. It is not as if Singapore is the only place where doctors can practice and the Singapore brand in healthcare is formidable. The greatest irony of the current rounds of manpower curtailing would be if in two to three decades, our successors are confronted with wanton pricing in specialties where there has been government-created scarcity and providers free to price willy nilly!

Healthcare is a complex adaptive system even in the best of times. In these times of unprecedented demographic and epidemiologic challenges and fiscal uncertainty, policy makers would be wise to beware unintended consequences. "Primum non nocere" — First do no harm.

Thank you very much.

Chapter 8

Race Relations in Singapore: Policies for the Management of Race and their Unintended Consequences

Mathew Mathews

Thank you David for the invitation to present some of my thoughts on the management of race relations in Singapore. I will be highlighting the issue of unintended consequences in this area of management. Unlike healthcare, the economy or matters of Smart Nation (which were discussed in previous sessions), where we often defer to expert opinion, we all have views about how race is to be managed. This complicates matters because our views of how race is to be managed is overly shaped by our personal experience.

Let me begin with an overview of the intention of race management policies. What do race management policies seek to achieve, not just locally but internationally? I must caution that the term race is not always used in other societies. Race is often viewed as a construct imposed on people by those in power. Some prefer terms like multicultural policies when speaking about race management. That is what I will be referring to — the whole slew of policies to deal with differences whether it is owing to race, ethnicity, religion, nationality or linguistic affiliation.

First, race management policies seek to reduce primordial differences and biases that exist in society. It also aims to unify the population. We can see how primordial differences, based on race, religion and language have played up in many parts of the world whether it is Sri Lanka, Bosnia or Indonesia. Even in Singapore, in our distant past, there were communal tensions which have turned violent. Such primordial differences have to be downplayed if any nation is to be cohesive and its population feeling a shared identity.

Second, race management policies try to reduce race-based exclusion and discrimination. This is a reality in many nations and detrimental to both individual and societal well-being.

Third, especially in societies which consider themselves multicultural, there is an attempt to use race management policies to celebrate cultural diversity.

Singapore has a several policies for the management of race. We have a multiracial framework constituting what is often referred to as the CMIO model (Chinese, Malay, Indian, Others). This has often been represented as four concentric circles, each one attributed to a race category. The areas where the concentric circles converge, represent our common space — we speak English, we go through similar life events, men go to National Service. We share experiences which are quite similar. But each racial group has its own peculiarities. This is represented in the outer non-overlapping parts of the circles.

We also have policies to ensure minority representation and well-being. Policies such as the GRCs (Group Representative Constituencies) guarantee minority representation in Parliament. More recently the reserved election for the President ensures that we will have a President of a minority race from time to time, even if our current system of election is not able to produce such a President from one of the constituent races in Singapore. We also have self-help groups, which try to uplift those in different communities who are not doing well using culturally appropriate methods to do so.

Race management strategies also entail that we have policies to help nudge intercultural interaction. This is based on the premise that we have a preference for those from our own communities. Thus, there needs to be mechanisms in place to force us out of our comfort zones to interact with other. There is the HDB (Housing Development Board) Ethnic Integration Policy, for instance, where there are race quotas in public housing to ensure that in every precinct, Singaporeans will be able to meet people of other races.

We also have programmes like the Inter-Racial and Religious Confidence Circles (IRCCs). This ensures that our religious and community leaders communicate with one another and build trust.

Finally, Singapore has in place legal measures, which serves as a deterrent to those who try to undermine the type of racial and religious harmony that Singaporeans are proud of. The Sedition Act, the Internal Security Act and the Maintenance of Religious Harmony Act are well known to us.

There are several effects of these different race management policies. Before I look at the negative unintended consequence, it is important to stress that there are many positive consequences that come out of Singapore's race management policies.

First, these policies have increased the sensitivity of our population to the reality of the diversity in our midst. We learn to respect and be sensitive to those of different backgrounds. Based on the IPS-OnePeople.sg Indicators of Racial and Religious Harmony, a random, representative survey of over 4000 respondents, which I led in 2013, we found that the large majority of Singaporeans embraced diversity. Around 70% of the respondents believed that it was good for Singapore to be made up of different races. We also did very well on various other indicators such as the relative absence of reported racial and religious tension. Discrimination based on race while experienced by some minorities at the work setting, was relatively absent when people used public services. Only 10% of racial minorities reported that they had ever felt that they were treated differently in a public service context — whether it is by the courts, the police, family service centres, or other public institutions.

Second, race management policies have made it necessary for Singaporeans to engage in cross-cultural interactions and in the process make accommodations. Based on the Channel News Asia-IPS Survey on Race Relations, which was conducted in 2016, most Singaporeans have interacted with those of other races in various settings. While it is not possible to assess the depth of these interactions, for all practical purposes this has allowed Singaporeans of different racial backgrounds to feel a sense of normality as they navigate through a multiracial society.

That brings me to the third point, which is that race management policies have made Singapore a much more appealing site for migration. Based on the IPS Community Leaders Integration Dialogue, quite a few immigrants in Singapore marvel at the fact that Singapore is able to preserve social cohesion despite the apparent diversities in the city state. The way that Singapore deals with diversity is something they applaud, and which makes them view Singapore as a good place to stay in and contribute.

Having presented the positive consequences of race management policies, let me now move to some of what some have argued are negative unintended consequences of our race management policies. I will talk about three of them — (1) racial categorisation; (2) safeguards to minority representation; and (3) the swift action by the government on racial and religious infractions.

Some of the drawbacks of racial categorisation include the entrenching of racial schemas, excluding some identities and relegating those who hold these identities to feel that they are "others", reducing a sense of national identity, and stifling adaptive cultural and demographic shifts. Let me give some examples. The IPS Survey of Race, Religion and Language released in 2014 found that a substantial proportion of Singaporeans say that their race is important or very important to their overall sense of identity. That itself is not problematic. However since we accentuate race so much in our society and discourse, does race then become an important schema we use to understand the people around us. Sometimes using race as a schema in some daily situations is not problematic — for instance, we recognise that someone is a Malay and may be careful about offering him non-Halal food since we associate Malays with Islam (and the dietary restrictions expected in Islam). But racial schemas can also result in racial stereotypes and prejudices in how we assess others. For example, the CNA-IPS survey found that stereotypes were held among a substantial proportion of Singaporeans. For instance, nearly half of our respondents to our survey agreed to statements such as "People from some races are more violent than others" and "People from some races are more likely to get into trouble than others".

The problem with relying on racial lenses when we assess people is that we often neglect that there are other socio-economic factors that are crucial to understanding people's behaviour. For instance, we may make misattributions on certain behaviour. We see someone or a group not performing well in Mathematics. We then misattribute this to culture or genetic predisposition based on the group's race. In reality the poor performance in Mathematics could be due to a lack of financial resources which has led to an inability to cope in a school system which uses a rigorous Mathematics syllabus.

Racial categorisation is also problematic because of how it excludes some ethnic identities which could otherwise be very meaningful to people. We have come a long way though. In the early days, Eurasians were often referred to as "Others" in state categorisation systems. Today, there is more recognition of the Eurasian label and the term and community is well recognised. But there have been times when people are not able to be classified into the racial identity that they believe is most congruent to their identity. Those with mixed parentage have to be categorised racially in a way which may not be meaningful to them.

Take the case of someone whose great grandfather was ab Indian who had married a Chinese woman and their subsequent generations married Chinese partners. Most likely, based on administrative systems, this person will still be considered Indian, though very little "Indianness" now resides in him. Of course, there are more options now with the government allowing since a few years ago for parents to select double-barrelled race options for their children.

Another potential problem of race categorisation is that it reduces one's sense of national identity. You may lose your sense of belonging to the nation if you are not part of the CMI (Chinese, Malay, Indian) or Eurasian category. Based on a series of focus group discussions we have done, those classified as Others such as those of Japanese, Filipino or Myanmar descent in Singapore feel that to really be Singaporean, then you have to be part of the major CMI or E categories. There is the assumption that if one does not fit into these major categories, it is hard for people to see you as legitimately Singaporean. To compound that, Singapore has a system of ethnic self-help to deal with the needs of those in the different communities who may be underperforming. This further entrenches the fact that belonging to a recognised, racial community is crucial if you want to be fully integrated into Singapore. This might stifle the development of a strong sense of national identity given the cultural and demographic shifts which might happen in Singapore with inter-marriages. In the long term, racial categories tend to be static. We however need to have fluidity to accommodate many of the changes that we will encounter culturally and demographically.

The second negative consequence of race management policies relate to safeguards for minority representation.

Some of these might limit the potential of minorities. For example, minorities might be seen as having insufficient merit to being elected for public office. They are supposed to need help to compete, as can be seen through the institution of the reserved election for the President or the Group Representative Constituencies. Some minorities can be elected on their own merit since they have the needed charisma to prevail even with the disadvantage of competing with a majority member candidate. So we may have the unintended consequence where some among the majority may question whether any minority in a high position is really there because he is a token. This then undermines the minority person's personal qualifications.

Related to the elections, as can be seen during the debates about the restricted elected President, there is the consequence where some, appealing to the CMIO framework believe that their racial group needs to be represented no matter how small their community is. We then have the unintended consequence of a certain kind of entitlement in terms of representation, where people believe that their group must be accorded certain top positions if they are going to be fully accepted as Singaporean.

Finally, there is the problem of swift government management on race issues. We have seen, time and time again, how the government is the most important player when it comes to the management of race and religion. This can however reduce community involvement. Many Singaporeans we surveyed in the IPS Survey of Race, Religion and Language believe that the government is responsible to ensure proper management of racial and religious issues. Similarly more than 60% feel that as a responsible citizen they should report racial and religious infractions to the authorities, apparently believing that this is something which the authorities should intervene in. Such an attitude has a way of dampening community involvement by leaving matters like this to the State rather than the community. We know for instance that when someone says something nasty about another race, the government can be depended on to take swift action. But we have no idea of how these prejudices, stereotypes and misunderstandings are to be challenged. Because of the speed of state action, we do not have opportunities to embark on a community driven approach to dispel myths and challenge prejudices. In fact, because of swift government action and how race management is often relegated as a sensitive matter, there is a fear about discussing issues surrounding race and religion. The CNA-IPS Survey on Race Relations showed that about 66% of Singaporean say that talking about racial issues causes unnecessary tension. We prefer to confine ourselves to the OB (out-of-bound) markers and be safe and not discuss issues which relate to race and religion. Even if there are things which bother us, we prefer to maintain a veneer of harmony or tolerance and not deal with the root issues. So essentially our stereotypes and prejudices still prevail though we are silent about them.

In conclusion, although the criticisms of current race management policies are valid, we have to evaluate these within the broader outcomes that current management strategies achieve. Many indicators of racial and religious harmony in Singapore are very positive. So the question one has to answer is whether we should ditch the current system or merely work to tweak some parts of the current working system. If we depend on the natural processes of societal development, which many academics call for in terms of the management of race relations, is it likely that the better angels — the good part of our nature — will prevail?

Thank you very much.

Chapter 9

Panel Discussion 3

Panelists: Jeremy Lim, Mathew Mathews
Moderator: Paulin Straughan

Paulin: David asked me to moderate two very diverse talks, but of course they are linked. In a way, the synergy is very clear. Both speakers dealt with emerging social concerns for Singapore society. One has to do with healthcare costs and the management of healthcare at a period when we are going to need intervention more than any time in the history of Singapore. And the other has to do with the notion of multiculturalism and how do we preserve it in order to ensure that we do not lose the essence of what makes and demarks Singapore, and at the same time not fragment us. I will begin with a question for Jeremy. On one hand, you talked about a glut in the supply of medical doctors but at the same time you said price is going up. Given the economics of supply and demand, why does it not ultimately result is some kind of adjustment on cost?

Jeremy: Well, if you look at the information technology industry, more computing power has been obtained despite lower costs. But if you look at health, the more sophistication or advances you have, the more healthcare costs go up; the more doctors you have, the more healthcare costs go up. It seems to be quite an intractable challenge. I think that there are fundamentally four different drivers. Let me just quickly run through them.

The first is that it is very human that our health can always get better and so when discretionary income goes up, we are always prepared to spend more. There is always that extra bit that you can do and there will always be a doctor willing to sell you the extra bit.

The second relates to this notion of consumerisation and the fact that I want it for myself customised, and I want it now. In the old days, patients were very happy to queue and so productivity of the doctor was very high — very little downtime as patients were the one queuing, and we did not measure patients' time spent waiting and we did not factor in the costs of this waiting and loss of productivity. So we had a very 'productive' healthcare system. But now we increasingly have to organise doctors around patients. This results in more redundancy and more inefficiency in the usage of your most important asset or your most expensive resource in the healthcare system, which is the doctors' time.

Third, we do have regulations. Take for example, the need to bring your foreign domestic worker, every six months, to the GP (general practitioner) to have a medical check. There are about two hundred thousand foreign domestic workers, and this adds up to four hundred thousand visits a year for essentially healthy women. We have almost a million foreign workers in this country in manual construction. Every year they go for a test and these tests must be done by a doctor, and that is a million additional consultations. You could not walk into a lab casually and say I want to have my cholesterol tested — they will ask you where is the doctor's order. So regulations, for better or worse, keep the system on a very even keel.

Lastly is around financing. Healthcare costs has gone up dramatically but the number of care episodes has not increased as much. So a lot of the rise in healthcare costs has been due to an increase in the unit cost. Well, when you remove the kind of stabilising power which used to be the insurer, which is the government, then we have a kind of market mechanism where unintended consequences can and do happen. One of these consequences in the healthcare system has been the ability on the part of doctors and other healthcare providers to price whatever they want to. For all these reasons, it is a happy situation if you are a well-established doctor. But if you are a patient, things can be better.

Paulin: But the market should correct for it, right? If you charge a thousand dollars and he charges a hundred, and both of you are equally qualified, why would I go to you and not him?

Jeremy: But you do not know that we are equally qualified. You cannot tell quality and therefore you take price as a surrogate for quality. Would you go to a thousand dollar doctor or the ten dollar doctor? You will say my health is worth more than ten dollars so I better go to the thousand dollar doctor. So that is the first perversion. The second perversion comes in when you say my employer is paying, so if there is a ten thousand dollar doctor, I will be happy to go to the ten thousand dollar doctor because someone else is paying. And that is the notion of moral hazard or the buffet syndrome.

Paulin: Thank you, Jeremy. Questions?

Audience Member #1: My question is for the whole panel although it is about race. I wonder whether the panel has thoughts about the unintended consequence of us not publicly reporting or discussing race issues, for example, public documents that will not give findings by race.

Mathew: From our survey, if you ask Singaporeans how they perceive race-based information and what kind of information should or should not be allowed, they seem to be happy with certain kind of race-based information being released. For instance, they are fine with health-based information being released. It is alright to say that Indians or Chinese die of certain diseases. People accept that because there is the notion that there are some biological predispositions of race. But when it comes to issues such as educational performance or social problems of a particular race, people feel more strongly and the number of people agreeing that such information should be released is very small. So I think we have this general idea that we should not talk about things which cast races in a negative light. Now, the bigger question is whether that is the best thing to do or not. Do we need to own some of those problems? One way of looking at it is that communities should own those problems. Take for example the problem about underperformance of a particular race. That was partly why the self-help group system came about because the issue was about underperformance of minority students. The idea is to let the community-based self-help group take care of that issue, let them try to correct it, let it be a community-owned problem. But of course the bigger issue comes in. If we see ourselves as Singaporean, then every person in Singapore who lags behind should be a concern and interest for all of us. But I think our policymakers feel that many Singaporeans may not be able to handle this kind of information about race and deal with the associated issues. It is not just the policymakers but many Singaporeans who feel that talking about race is going to bring about discomfort.

Jeremy: I think there is a certain security blanket when we talk about race in the context of science. So we say Indians or Chinese have a certain health risk and so on. But I am a bit uncomfortable with that for two reasons. One is about the utilisation of scarce public resources. Let us take smoking rates. They are disproportionately high in certain ethnic groups amongst males. Does Singapore has a smoking problem nationally? No, we do not, at least not to the same degree across genders and ethnicities. Do we have a smoking issue with certain ethnic groups of a certain age and gender profile? Yes, we do. But our campaigns tend to be national because we do not want to target races. But a lot of the campaigning in public health and so on could arguably be called deadweight financing because we are not hitting the right population.

The part where I am less comfortable is really around overly simplistic depiction of issues as being rooted in single causes such as ethnicity . We talked about under educational performance of certain ethnic groups. I would go look at the statistics of infant mortality rates. Between races there could be a two to three times difference. Is it medical? You could argue so but it is clear that the social determinants of health are huge factors in explaining why certain ethnic groups have two to three times the infant mortality rates that the others have. If we approach this narrowly from the lens of a scientific issue and say there must be a gene that explains this, I think we are barking up the wrong tree.

Paulin: I totally agree with Jeremy, and I mean my discomfort with placing too much on racial categories. One, race is not a homogenous entity. If you look within the Indian community, it is not homogeneous and it is the most diverse category. Second, precisely because of our deep appreciation of the social determinants and fundamental causes of diseases and poverty and so on, we know that race is only of the many measures of culture.

Audience Member #2: We all want more data available, but I am very sad to see the ethnicity of diabetes reported in The Straits Times. It gives people part of the story and they say "Ah, it's race." In Singapore, the distribution of income sadly follows race. Now, the lowest income group in Singapore society will have enough problems that cluster with income. And when income corresponds to ethnicity, you get a very dangerous situation where people blame the race rather than the fact that these people are in that particular income group.

Paulin: So this syndrome of blaming the victim.

Audience Member #2: Yes. Let people have all the information. It would not matter they would realise that income was behind it or not. But when they only have part of the information, which is race, they say the problem is related to race. I have seen that in so many committees where people have not had the full information. That I think is very unfortunate and it gives us more problems to deal with.

Audience Member #3: My question is for Matthew. You left us dangling with a question and I thought I remind you. You said "If we depend on the natural processes of societal development, is it likely that the better angels will prevail?" I would like to find out your answer to that question that you posed.

Mathew: I think one can accuse me of having a dim view of human beings though I generally do not. But if you look at the empirical facts in terms of how people view race, then at least at this point in time we still hold on to quite a few stereotypes. Discrimination and prejudice also exist. There are stereotypes that I believe are deep-seated and partly because we have never been able to talk a lot about these things. We seldom try to find out why people have certain perceptions. People need to be educated that there are many other things that may have resulted in a particular group of people being in the criminal justice system, and it may not just be about their culture but because of many other issues. So in that sense, I would say we still have some way to go and it seems to me that natural processes of societal development may not bring about the desired effect. Maybe there might be some kind of change about a decade or two later. So we should wait and see.

Audience Member #4: I like to take up the question that you (Matthew) just answered — if you let things be, will our better angels emerge and settle things. I must say I share your thoughts that I do not think if we leave things naturally things will fall into place. I think here in Singapore we do manage diversity, and you can nudge, you can shape, you can prevent ghettoisation. But Matthew, do you think our curriculum in school can better prepare our students for multicultural living? We do not talk about race but do we understand the history and the cultural characteristics of each of the dominant populations and communities? And can we work in some way of teaching and celebrating diversity even of a group that we have not yet encountered?

Mathew: It happens that I did review the social studies syllabus used in our schools. One of the things that I have been calling for has been a willingness of people to be able to talk about race. Sadly, our educators are part of the system and they themselves find it very difficult to approach issues to do with race. They say that anytime you openly discuss race issues, if it is not the politically correct kind of talk about race, it is bound to lead to trouble. There are concerns that students will go back home and relate what they heard to their parents. This may generate a parent complaint and the principal might haul them (the teacher) up in the process. It then becomes very difficult for teachers to discuss racial issues because of the potential sensitivities. With the new social studies curriculum being a little bit broader in scope, teachers have more free play. But what the teachers have is still comparatively only a very small amount of resource when it comes to discussing race. I believe that the Ministry of Education is trying to enhance this part of the curriculum to give students greater cultural competencies to navigate the 21st century. I think that will be a good thing.

Paulin: Mathew, this whole discourse on race follows a very traditional approach towards race relations where we assume that we can talk about CMIO. Looking forward, we are trying to future proof Singapore in terms of race. Surely the deconstruction of 'O' has to take centre stage. I think if we start to deconstruct 'O' and frame it positively in a language of inclusiveness, I believe young Singaporeans would be very excited. Do you agree?

Mathew: I believe the CMIO categories are important. They have administrative purposes and I do not believe we should get rid of them. But we need to change how we conceptualise and see people, and be able to say that people have valid ethnic identities which should be celebrated. We want to give people due respect and recognition to their choice of ethnic identity as much as possible. But we are some way from that because we are still at the stage where it is about deciding which neat little boxes to put people in. I think we have to grow to be able to accept that kind of diversity.

Jeremy: Please permit me to tie this obsession with putting things into neat little boxes and what we shared earlier about complex adaptive systems. One of our challenges as a country is that we always want to get it right. At least in a complex adaptive system such as health and probably race as well, it is less about getting it right and more about not getting it irreversibly wrong. It is about having that 'system flex' so that we can change course. I think that is what has allowed Singapore to successfully navigate the first 50 years, and I do believe that is what will allow us to navigate the next 50 years. But critical to that is our ability to learn and our ability to talk about where we have gone wrong. I would say that the Singapore health story has been one of immense success but have we lived up to our fullest, to our very fullest potential? The answer is probably no.

Paulin: Jeremy, you talked about gatekeepers and third party administrators who seem to play a regulatory kind of role without which you fear that cost could escalate. So my question then is what about this very big group of Allied Health Professionals. How do they feature in your equation?

Jeremy: I think they are related questions. If we look at a chronic disease such as diabetes, it is now focused mainly on taking your medicine and seeing your doctor regularly. But far more important are our lifestyle and diet changes. And that is the part that we doctors are horrendously bad. We are good at being paternalistic and protectionist, but we are not good at empathy and spending time to understand the disease in the context of the patients' worldview and environment. That is what virtually every other healthcare professionals does better but they are often not enabled or empowered to do so because of regulatory constraints. The channel has to go through the doctor as the gatekeeper. Many times that is beneficial but many times that is also detrimental. It drives up cost and it prevents patients from getting the care that they need because the doctors become the bottleneck. There is a health system in the United States that is called Iora Health, where the doctor works with a team of nurses and what they call health coaches. These health coaches are the ones who spend a lot of time with patients whether the chronic disease is mental health related, diabetes, and so on. It is a much more efficient model because the doctor does what the doctor does best, which is on the clinical therapeutic side, and the health coaches do what they do best. What is the background of these health coaches? They could be gym instructors, yoga teachers, and so on. I think that is the sort of model that our regulations and our healthcare financing systems will need to allow. Hopefully some of these lessons can diffuse back to Singapore and we can adapt them to fit local use.

Audience Member #5: I have never heard anyone mention traditional medicine in this whole panoply of solutions. There are many other alternative medicine that are very effective and mostly cost free or low cost. Why is it that in Singapore sitting in the confluence of two or three great civilisations, we never ever talk about the Chinese or Indian or Malay traditional medicine as part of the solution?

Jeremy: We have grown up since the British colonial days with a predominantly western view of medicine. When this western view became entrenched through our education system and our regulation, it essentially crowded out everyone. And because healthcare is almost always funded by a third party (insurer, employers), it has been difficult for TCM (Traditional and Complementary Medicine) to flourish. But despite all that, many Singaporeans pay out of their own pocket to see traditional and complementary medicine providers. In fact, studies have shown that at least 80% of patients who are undergoing cancer treatment with a western provider will also be taking supplements and other medicines. So I would say that there is a very legitimate role for non-western medicine. It has not been able to thrive partly because of regulatory and financing reasons, but also partly because of the scientific paradigm. The western scientific paradigm is a very reductionist one and that is not the lens that you can view TCM. But because that is the only lens that regulators have, TCM just does not make the mark. And if it cannot be regulated, it cannot be financed, and therefore it cannot live up to its fullest potential.

Paulin: Jeremy and Mathew are leaders in their field, so I am privileged to have moderated this session. Please thank them and thank you very much.

Part IV

Chapter 10

Closing Panel Discussion: Unintended Consequences in Singapore

Panelists: David Chan, Chan Heng Chee, Han Fook Kwang, Kishore Mahbubani
Moderator: Tommy Koh

Tommy: Thank you all very much for staying for the final panel. David, a good friend, is very persuasive and every year he persuaded me to chair the closing panel for him. This is a wonderful panel, I could not be happier with the four panelists. The agreement among all five of us is that each of them will make a five-minute initial statement. I will ask each of them one question and then open it to all of you for questions. So, I begin with Heng Chee.

Heng Chee: Thank you, Tommy, and also thanks to Arnoud and David. Singapore prides itself as a long term planning state, and we are admired internationally for it. We even have this term "Whole-of-Government", which presumably improves performance. We think through our problems, so technically, we should never have unintended consequences, right? But of course, that is not true.

The biggest unintended consequence for Singapore is the separation of Singapore from Malaysia. After we worked so hard to merge with Peninsula Malaysia, the unintended consequences ended with our leaving the Federation. I think it was unintended on Malaysia's part also. But the point is, we were able to make a success of independent Singapore. Brexit for Britain was unintended consequences for David Cameron but the "leave" voters would say it was intended consequences. So, it can be unintended for one side and intended for the other. I think the main point is that the only thing you can do when you have arrived at unintended consequences is to get out of it, to make the best of a bad deal. And I would say, thankfully, I cannot remember any more spectacular unintended consequences that we have faced in Singapore since separation. We had unintended consequences but they were not as spectacular as separation. I can just name a few.

First, immigration in Singapore is intended to increase population because Singapore as a small country needs more people. Unintended — negative backlash. Too many came in too short a time and calling the policy "foreign talent" was extremely negative. We were not coordinated. But you can correct that policy and I think the government is now trying to do that, with fewer numbers each time staggering it. I think numbers do make a difference. Immigration is an issue for many other countries as well today, and one has to be very careful about the numbers coming in, whether it is Europe or the United States. Certainly in Europe — if one million people go to Germany as refugees, there are unintended consequences.

Second issue — our universities. We seek to internationalise our universities and we have them ranked and we are now doing very well. Our universities NUS (National University of Singapore) and NTU (Nanyang Technological University) are top ranked and that is a good thing. The unintended consequence of this internationalisation is the loss of the Singapore national core in the studies and research focus, and also the character of the university. We are certainly in danger because "Singapore studies" is not very much the fashion now, and universities are the intellectual seats of our country. I think we will try to do something about it, but it is going to be a long walk back.

The third unintended consequence is in healthcare. Medisave is a good thing but the unintended consequence is you have a bed crunch because we have medisave — people have money to stay longer in the hospital. I think the Medisave scheme allows families to keep themselves and their loved ones in the hospital for a longer time than necessary. These are unintended consequences and maybe someone can work this out.

So these are some lighter unintended consequences. The question I have, going forward, is how do we prepare ourselves as Singaporeans for situations of unintended consequences? How do we anticipate, and if we can anticipate it is no longer unintended consequences. That is the irony. And if we prepare ourselves, what do we prepare for? I think technological change is a big thing. That is the one we all know but it is the hardest to anticipate.

There is another point I want to talk about. Do we prepare ourselves for the day when Singapore's geo-strategic position is threatened or changed by technological change? Think Hawaii. Honolulu used to be a great stopping point on the way to the United States. Came the long haul planes and suddenly Honolulu is bypassed. So we now have a good geo-strategic location. Will technological change in some ways impact it? And how to prepare ourselves for the day when our neighbours become real competitors of Singapore. How do we react to that?

Finally, I just want to ask this question. What are the qualities to deal with unintended consequences?

I would say, first, we have to be nimble. The word is used all the time but what does it mean to be nimble? How do we become nimble? Can we learn to be nimble or are we born nimble? Maybe it is a little of both. But the most important thing is for us to recognise the unintended consequence when it hits us. In other words, you have a problem, accept it, admit it and start changing it. But if you don't, it just drags on. So I think as Singaporeans, as bureaucrats, as policymakers, as managers, or executives of companies, we have to realise we hit something we did not prepare for, diagnose the problem, change it, and accept it.

Secondly, I think in organisations, particularly in bureaucracies, there must be more robust internal discussions on policies and thinking through consequences, and having these robust discussions with a wider range of people — not the same sets of people. You really need people with different backgrounds to think about what could happen especially in a VUCA (volatile, uncertain, complex, ambiguous) world. We tend to be talking to the same few people. We come from the same universities and everybody has the same background. We need to talk to a diversity of people.

Finally, to prepare for unintended consequences, we need naysayers in the leadership team who can think the unthinkable. In preparing ourselves for unintended consequences, we really need leadership. That is what it is about.

Tommy: Thank you Heng Chee. Kishore, you are next.

Kishore: Thank you Tommy. Let me begin by congratulating Arnoud and David for organising this spectacular conference. I am very happy to be here at this final panel. I am going to carry on the theme that Heng Chee started of talking about successful public policies in Singapore and their unintended consequences. I will talk about three of the most successful public policies of Singapore. Number one, our car policy. Number two, our civil service. Number three is about our culture of realism — Singapore prides itself on being the most realistic country in the world.

In theory, our car policy works, right? We raised the prices so high and made it very difficult for most of the population to own cars, and so you do not have traffic jams like in Kuala Lumpur, Jakarta, Bangkok and so on. So it is a success. But one of the unintended consequences of raising the prices so high is that you've made the car such a treasured object in Singapore society. I can assure you that if you look at the behaviour of Singaporeans, there is a very active cult of car worship in Singapore. When I go running in the morning in my neighbourhood, what do I see? These foreign domestic workers waking up at 6.30 am and polishing their employers' cars. Car ownership is such an important part of the identity of being a Singaporean. You must have a car if you have arrived.

But paradoxically, that success has now become our biggest liability. What is happening in other cities is that many people are making very sensible, rational decisions that if you have a smartphone and you can get an Uber or a Grab taxi, you do not need to own a car anymore. If you want to go from point to point, most of the time you can get by without car ownership. In Manhattan, for example, it is perfectly normal not to own cars. But in Singapore, where the cost per year of using Uber to get from point to point is so much cheaper than owning a car, and where it is therefore irrational to own a car, you've created this culture of car worship. The unintended consequence of our car policy is that we cannot reduce the car population anymore. So that is one unintended consequence.

The second is our civil service. I can very proudly say that our civil service is one of the best in the world. There is no question whatsoever. It helps that it is also one of the best paid in the world. I know it helps, but the unintended consequence — and this is of course a very sensitive point — is that we do not have a private sector that is one of the best in the world. Why is that?

I think it has to do, in part, with the fact that the civil service sucks away the best brains in Singapore at the age of eighteen and promises them all kinds of wonderful scholarships. And before you know it, they have all hitched the wagon to the public sector. The public sector is so comfortable, and by the time you are thirty, if you are good, you are earning three hundred thousand dollars a year. Why would you want to quit and do something risky, right? And so that is clearly an unintended consequence. But more dangerously, it also means that whenever you are thinking of solutions to problems, you always think, "Oh, the public sector must solve it". And frankly, as you saw in the case of Uber and Grab, we could not fix our taxi problem. But somebody invented Uber and suddenly you can get from point to point in a heavy rain storm with surge pricing in Uber. That is the private sector. The most brilliant civil servants could not think of it — surge pricing.

My third point is the culture of realism, and this again is one of Singapore's biggest strengths. One of the miracles of Singapore is that we have gone through fifty years without experiencing war. By the way, if you look at most countries that became independent in or around 1965, most of them have experienced some kind of war or conflict. We have not. Our realism works.

But Singaporeans have, unfortunately because of the culture of realism, confused realism with cynicism, and they believe the way to show you are realistic is to show how cynical you are. To give you one obvious example, this year we are celebrating ASEAN's 50th anniversary and that is why I am launching a book in two weeks' time on ASEAN. But I find that, in trying to market ASEAN to Singaporeans, they are realistic and therefore cynical and so they rubbish ASEAN. Now, the Singaporeans are the single biggest beneficiaries of the ecosystem of peace that ASEAN has created. We are the biggest beneficiaries because we are the most globalised country in the world. Our total trade is four times the size of our GNP (Gross National Product) and we can only do that because of ASEAN. And nobody in Singapore thanks ASEAN. Worse still, because of the culture of cynicism, we are strangling the ASEAN secretariat when we should be feeding it and strengthening it. When realism leads to cynicism, that is a very painful unintended consequence.

Tommy: I think Kishore has lived up to his reputation for being provocative. He made three very good points. We will tackle him in a short while. Fook Kwang, could you share with us five minutes of wisdom?

Fook Kwang: Thanks Tommy, and thanks for inviting me to this panel. I am going to go around the universe before I get to my point.

Earlier this week, I attended a fascinating talk by a world-renowned cosmologist John Barrow of Cambridge University on the origin of the universe. One of the most interesting points he made in the talk was that we are living in a period in the evolution of the universe, which is very fortuitous for the emergence of life including intelligent life. The universe is 13.8 billion years old. It is amazing how this scientist can actually measure the age of the universe but it is only during this period that, apparently according to the theory, life can exist. If it is too early, you have no time for the important elements to be formed. You know the metallic elements including carbon. If it is too late, most of the stars including the sun would have exhausted the energy and they would have collapsed into a white dwarfs or red dwarfs or whatever and life would not have been able to exist. So it is only this period, give or take a hundred million years, that life can emerge. So perhaps it is also true in the case of nations. There are only certain periods in nationhood where something can happen, and in the case of Singapore, the first 50 years was very fortuitous for rapid economic development. We are newly emerging country, we have no resources, we dared to do many things without thinking of the unintended consequences.

I will just mention some of the bold things that we made — introducing national service and daring to house eighty-five percent of the population in public housing. Can you imagine the logistics involved? And introducing the English language as our working language when eighty to ninety percent of the people did not speak the language and could not string a complete sentence of English together.

Now we are more developed and much more successful, with lots of resources. But I think one unintended consequence of having been so successful in so short a time is that we have become too risk-adverse and we inherited a sort of a "settled" mindset. We briefly mentioned this in the opening panel session. Perhaps it has to do with the institutionalisation of organisations. It has to do with fearing that we will lose it all if you make a major mistake. It has to do with many things including the way our organisations have developed. But I am very concerned about the inability or the unwillingness to take bigger risks with our policies, and I want to mention two areas.

One is in the field of education. We all know that in this brave new world, you need to be more innovative, more creative, more enterprising, and more risk-taking, and you need to change our education system to do this. To be fair to the government, I think they have done so. But I feel that the change has not been fast enough. As Boon Siong mentioned earlier this morning, why does it take six years to change the PSLE result system from a T-score to something else? It is going to take six years. I feel that some of the changes that we are going to implement is taking far too long.

The second area is the economy. We have been struggling quite a bit to get out of this slow growth period in which are in. Singapore has never encountered more than two years of slow growth in its entire fifty-year history. But this year, if the projection comes true, which is two to four percent, it would have been four years of slow growth since 2014. I see that we are beginning to accept two to four percent as the acceptable new normal and I have a problem with that. The reason why we accept two to four percent is that we looked at all the other developed and matured economies and we said at a certain point in the development you can only do two to four percent, and that the days of seven, eight and nine percent are over. But in the case of Singapore, despite the tremendous economic development that we have achieved, we do not have the same level of maturity and sophistication throughout our economy as you will find in Japan or Germany or the northern Scandinavian countries. There are many sectors of the economy in Singapore which are really still very third world, including many of our local SMEs (small and medium enterprises).

The other point is that we are a city-state, and I think cities are expected to grow much faster than larger countries. And that accounts for the dynamism of cities. So if we too prematurely accept two to four percent as the new normal from now on, I think there will be many unintended consequences.

Tommy: Thank you Fook Kwang. David, it is your turn.

David: Thanks Tommy. We have spoken a lot about unintended consequences. So let's abbreviate that as

"UC", for unintended consequences. Intended consequences is "IC". So, you see ("UC") and I see ("IC"). I really do not mean that as a joke. Every mission, every measure, and every intervention are all purposeful actions, and so they have an intended goal and therefore there must be an intended consequence. So the reason we have a new statutory board, or its goals, we will have to explain to the public, and we have to justify the use of public resources. So the goal or the purposive action provides you the IC — the intended consequences. Our problem now is as we move along being goal-focused, we forget about the unintended consequences. So you need to see the UC at the same time and not just see the IC.

But we also spoke about what happens if we get paralysed worrying too much about the unintended consequences, that then nothing will be done. Then there is also the policymaker counterpoint that you are always criticising me for the UC and what I have not done, but you don't see the good things that I have achieved. And you talk about the perverse effects, but what about the fact that actually I am making a trade-off decision and therefore we need to look at both IC and UC simultaneously all the time.

It is true that what we are trying to do in this conference is to awaken all of us because we are "too IC" that we forgot about the UCs. But I think ultimately we are trying to say "You see I see" and "I see you see", and then we begin to realise that it is about perspective-taking. Solutions can come about when I begin to see what you see, and you begin to see what I see. And if we want the social compact in the relationships involving the Government, the private sector, the public and academia and so on, you have to start looking at things from the another's perspectives. When you do so, their intended consequence could be your unintended consequence, and vice versa.

Now, when you start talking about it, you will realise that many of these intended and unintended consequences, especially the unintended one, can be positive and they need not be inherently negative. So you do not have to be too concerned that I am focusing on unintended consequences, thinking that I am being very negative and focusing only on the negatives.

Let me give you a quick example of a positive unintended consequence. From the Budget, you hear that we are going to have these small centres where people and organisations can come to, where you introduce them to Intellectual Property, technology, and so on. These are the so-called lower-level SMEs that you are trying to digitise, and help them survive and improve productivity. In fact, what you end up doing here is also bringing different people and organisations together who on their own will never meet. The consequence is you will find there the whole supply chain meeting and interacting, and there will be a lot of value add. You begin by going to this centre to try to learn or figure out something like IP or technology, and you end up meeting someone else also going there, and then that someone else actually can solve your problem and often much better than the civil servant sitting at the centre. Many of these problems to be solved are difficult for the staff at the centre who is from the public service sector who may not know enough about the issues in the private sector. So your centre initiative's intended consequences to digitise the SMEs may or may not be achieved but because the different SMEs, including the entire supply chain, are all coming to the same place and they interact, you end up having SMEs mutually solving some of their problems.

Now, that is a simple example of a positive unintended consequence. But if you give out a feedback form and you ask the SME, "Did the public servant at the centre help you or solve your problem?" Your feedback form results may not be very positive. Well, in a 5-point scale, maybe you get a score of 3 for the staff's help. Should you then terminate the centre or the initiative? No. Because you need to understand that there is a very positive consequence that you had not planned for. So if you ask the SMEs what did you gain from this experience of coming to the centre, the response will be very positive because some of their problems were solved and they possibly even obtained some new business opportunities. If you focus on the unintended consequences, you don't just see the negatives, you will begin to see the positive aspects too.

Another quick example. The Budget also talked about A*STAR giving expert help to a few hundred companies in the next few years. These are the more sophisticated SMEs where you can provide them high-level assistance, such as to help them internationalise. Apparently we are going to also allow them to have thirty-six months or so of free IP. In a sense, it is an extension of the previous example I gave. It is a good initiative and very worthwhile for the SMEs. They will have more time and resources, and I think some will really want to do it because it is financially very worth it. So these SMEs will end up doing well and doing better, and that is the goal or the intended consequence.

But there is also an unintended positive consequence. Now, the researchers in A*STAR are very smart people, and they tend to be more practice-oriented than most professors in the universities because they have to spend a lot of time interacting with industries and meeting the economic KPIs (key performance indicators). But many of them are fresh PhDs. There are both foreigners and Singaporeans, and there are scholars who just completed their doctoral studies and they have not really worked out there in the workplace. When they start interacting with these companies and helping them as part of the A*STAR initiative, they will begin to better understand how their expertise and technology can solve important practical real-world problems. They will become very problem-driven, and their next research project on simulation will be much more realistic in the parameters that they put into the simulation model. In this example, the development of translational abilities and interest among our researchers is an important unintended consequence of the initiative that is positive. I do not think that when this initiative was planned in the Budget we were already thinking of how to make A*STAR researchers more practice-oriented or translational. But it will happen and it will be an unintended consequence that is a positive one.

Let me end my comments with that part of the Budget that talked about the regulatory sandbox where you remove or suspend some regulations as an experiment. I think there are potential negative unintended consequences to the regulatory sandbox that you in the audience should pay attention to because some of you may be in charge of a sandbox, because the sandbox practice is going to expand well beyond the MAS (Monetary Authority of Singapore) and the area of finance. What will happen is that, in the regulatory sandbox, we all actually don't want the experiment to fail. So if you are assigned to take care and monitor a sandbox, you have this unconscious or subconscious thought that goes, "We better make it work", because something good must come out of all the effort put into the sandbox, right? So what happens? You will be very nice to everybody participating in the regulatory sandbox. You provide them all the information and you help them a lot. You ask them what their problems are, you pre-empt their problems, and you them how to solve it or get more help, and so on. And your regulatory sandbox will end up working very well and you honestly thought that things will be good by removing the regulations. In fact, you have created an artificial sandbox. You have created a situation where you spent so much time with the person or company providing them the information in such a way that in the real world it cannot or will not happen. So you will have a sandbox that is very successful but not representative of the real world. It is not just about not scalable because you will not have enough resources in the real world to provide information or help. You have produced a contrived laboratory in the sandbox that is not ecologically valid and relevant to the real world. We must watch out for that. That will be an example of all good intentions ending up with a negative consequence, out of very good intentions of the civil servant trying to make it work. I think we need to be honest about these things, and then we will make a positive difference.

So, for ICs and UCs, think about "I see you see" and "You see I see", and then you begin to realise that you can then bring different people together and the diverse perspectives can be complementary to co-create solutions rather than be a problem.

Tommy: Thank you David. I am going to learn from Fook Kwang. This morning when you chaired the first panel, you asked Arnoud De Meyer and David Chan one question, "What is the one change you would like to see in Singapore?" I remember Arnoud's answer for that was he would like to see Singapore being much more open about our failures. And David's reply for that was he would like to see Singapore much more accepting of diversity of opinions and views. So I am going to ask you, Fook Kwang, if you can make one paradigm change in Singapore, what is that one change you would like to make?

Fook Kwang: I think there are many things. One change is the recognition of talent and the concept of meritocracy. I am not going to go into the argument about all the other types of talent we should recognise because I think that has been very well discussed. I will just narrow it down to this. We say that we practise meritocracy because we recognise talent and believe that is the best way of getting the best out of the person and of improving the society. But I think over time in Singapore we have also placed a very large premium, not just on the merit of the person or the organisation but also trustworthiness or dependability. And we feel that we need to put people in position of power or authority whom we have that level of trust and confidence, and also who are of that same mindset and worldview that we have constructed in the course of the last fifty years, so that we have a certain comfort level with him or her. I think in doing that we missed out on the potential of many other people and we missed out on a whole range of abilities, apart from those that we are very comfortable and we recognise. So I would like to see us being more enlightened and being more embracing of not just other abilities but other worldviews and other mindsets.

Tommy: Thank you. Kishore, you have given us three examples of success stories — our car policy, civil service and culture of realism — but in each case you have given us the negative unintended consequence. If you can make one paradigm change in Singapore, what would that be?

Kishore: There is one paradigm change that I would like to see and I would like to see in this room. Tommy, Heng Chee, Fook Kwang, David and I, we all speak all around the world. And I can tell you that I can smell a Singaporean audience. In so many places in the world, when you begin a discussion, immediately dozen hands in the audience go up and they ask questions and challenge and even sometimes rubbish the speaker. But it is always a struggle to get the first question in a Singapore audience. Why is that so? I think Singaporeans actually have not done enough reflection on why this is happening in Singapore. Why is it that we can't do something that is quite easy and natural in most societies? Which is to ask hard questions. And I can tell you — if I may say something that will get me into deep trouble — which unfortunately is a true fact, yes, there was a phase in Singapore's history when there was a culture of fear, but that era is gone. There is no longer a culture of fear in Singapore but during the period of the culture of fear, the culture of questioning also disappeared. So what we need to bring back into Singapore, in a very robust fashion, is a culture of questioning and challenging. So Heng Chee is absolutely right when she says we need more naysayers. It is so rare that you come to Singapore events where one person stands up and says that the entire panel is speaking rubbish. I mean, they may not think we are speaking rubbish, but at least challenge us. And frankly, I can tell you the biggest danger Singapore faces in the next fifty years is taking all the formulas of the first fifty years and applying them to the next 50 years. It is a different world, so we have to create completely new formulas, and you cannot create completely new formulas until you attack every sacred cow in Singapore and challenge it, and then we can succeed.

Tommy: I have a different explanation for the reluctance for Singaporeans to stand up and question the speaker. I think it is a legacy about Confucianist culture. Let me explain. I seriously believe it is a result of a legacy of this very deep civilisation of respect for the elders, of a very hierarchical worldview. I personally experienced this myself in one particular year when I was a visiting professor back-to-back at the Chinese University of Hong Kong and then in the following week I was at the Zhejiang University in Hangzhou. The Hong Kong students behaved just like the Singapore students. I could not get questions from them. So the questions posed to me were by their professors and guests. But when I went to next door to Hangzhou, and after I finished my lecture, there was a whole sea of hands asking me questions. I asked Professor Wang Gungwu to explain the difference. He said because the Cultural Revolution had destroyed this one aspect of Confucianist culture. Chinese students today are like American students.

They are uninhibited; they no longer have this deeply ingrained sense of respect for their teachers. So, our explanations may be different, the conclusions are the same. I agree with Kishore — we should encourage Singaporeans to question conventional wisdom and question authority, of course in a respectful way. So Heng Chee, I ask you the same question. If you can make one paradigm shift in Singapore, what is that one paradigm change you would make?

Heng Chee: So many things have been said and every point is valid. Arnoud, David, Fook Kwang, Kishore; I think we are all talking about the same things. There are many changes we need to make to the paradigm we now have. We are successful but we could be more successful, and that is the point. I want to make a point on speaking up. Tommy, I am not sure if it is Confucian. I thought maybe it is colonialism because Hong Kong was under colonial authority and so were we. When I was in school, I used to put my hand up all the time to answer questions and my classmates hated me. In Singapore, we do have this culture, but it is not just Singapore. Everywhere, the person who stands up and puts up the hand is not liked. As Ambassador in Washington, I went to many campuses in the United States. I went to Wharton and I spoke to the students. I asked a Singapore student, "Have you ever asked a question in class?" He said no, he has never asked a question in his class. I said, "Can you promise me one thing? By the end of this year, you would have asked one question in your class." I go to Harvard and there are Asian students and again, the Korean speaks up, the Indonesian speaks up. It could be fractured English but they still speak up. Chinese students too, they asked questions. Not a single Singapore student who sat in the room asked a question, and English is not their problem. That is the position we are in.

Now let me just answer your question — what is the paradigm shift I would like to see. Since others have said so many things, I would like to emphasise just one thing. I was going to make the point that Fook Kwang made about expanding the circle of acceptability, but I am saying now I wish to see Singaporeans take more initiative. I think it is very easy to blame the system, and we do not take initiative. We are always expecting someone else to do things to us. When two neighbours quarrel in a HDB (Housing Development Board) apartment, they go to the members in a block, they go to the MP (Member of Parliament) to get the problem resolved, and that is not good. We should try to solve things ourselves. And I have noticed that whenever there is somebody that stopped to do something for someone else, it is the foreign worker doing that. I have noticed that Malays in Singapore will do that as well. They stop and take initiative, and it is a positive thing.

Tommy: David, in addition to the answer you gave this morning, which is that one big change you want to see in Singapore is the acceptance of the diversity of opinions and views, what is the next big change you would like to see? The second big change?

David: What I am going to say now is related to directly answering Tommy's question. You have heard that Singaporeans not speaking up might be due to colonialism, due to Confucianism, and also due to fear of punishment.

Of course, you know that you are going to get a different answer from me, so that we get more diversity of views.

I think they are all possible explanations and we don't have to say that only one is right and the other is wrong — that is paradoxical thinking, it is not binary "either-or". So, as a behavioural scientist, I will offer you another explanation, which I think applies to many people. And that is the fear of looking bad. It is basically about fear of failure. There is actually a science of the fear of looking bad. It has been around for about twenty over years, MOE (Ministry of Education) actually knows this very well, and it has to do with the different types of goal orientations.

When you want to do something, you have a goal. Your goal could be to impress others, and that is called a "prove performance goal" — you are trying to prove to others your ability and performance, that you are good. Then there is also an "avoid performance goal". You want to not speak up, because you know that you are going to look bad, or not intelligent, when you speak up. You are avoiding performance. And finally there is a "learning performance goal", which is that you want to learn from errors and understand not just what goes wrong but why, and you want to master the subject matter. Now, we are lacking in this learning or mastery goal orientation. We tend to be very good in the prove performance goal — we want to be the "A" student, and you want to be a First Class honours to prove that you are better than the Second Upper's. But we are also very avoid performance goal oriented. Now, this is not about being "Kiasu" or afraid to lose. So don't confuse them.

Once you understand this research on different types of goal orientation, which has been around for many years, you then begin to understand why your PSLE need to move from the T-score to the grade banding — because it was the T-score and its decimal, zero-sum competitive ranking that is reinforcing the performance goal orientations, at the expense of learning goal orientation. What it does is that the only way you can do well is you must be better than me. Therefore, I must do worse than you, otherwise you can't be good, and that is what psychometricians refer to as norm-referenced tests. But when we adopt a learning goal orientation, we do not focus or think about the bell curve or ranking competition. How do I master the subject? Whether I can master and whether you can master is independent of each other. But if you think in terms of competitive curve, you start saying that I want to prove that I am better than you, or I want to make sure I am not worse than you. So I think it is this system of reinforcing the performance goal orientations rather than the learning orientation, which is a very different concept from respect for authority, fear of punishment, or colonialism. I don't disagree that these three factors, at a macro level, could partially explain some aspects of not speaking up. But at the individual psychological level, I think avoid performance goal is important and operating when people don't or won't speak up.

If you are in the civil service, you will know exactly what I am about to say next. When we worked together on an issue, you talked so much to me. But when the Minister was present, you were completely quiet. And then when we were together again, and I said, "Why don't you speak up?" Then you spoke up and gave wonderful views, and so I said, "Why didn't you speak up?"

And then you said, "Yeah, I may look bad you know?" I think it is the fear of looking bad, whatever bad means, and this happens to very competent people. In fact, the more competent you are and the more successes you have, the more you want to avoid performance situations where you will or may look bad.

So the one thing I really want about paradigm change is related to this, and that is, forget about how intelligent you are. And even forget about your prescribed role, and step up to speak up. You know, if I just stick to my role as a professor, I will not be writing newspaper articles. I am not a Straits Times journalist and my job role is not to write newspaper articles. They do not add to my academic performance and recognition. If I just stick to my academic role, then I should just teach my students, publish my research in top journals, give academic talks and enjoy the academic prestige of impressing other academics. But if I think that I have a useful view on societal or public issues and I don't write a newspaper article because that is not my job role, or because I worry about offending the Government or the opposition, and so I just hope that someone else will express my view, then no one is better off. So my suggestion, and what I want to see change in Singapore, is for more people to step up to speak up, even if it outside their role. Because if you love the country, the role is less important than what matters. It is not that you respect your role less, but you should love the country more.

Tommy: Thank you David. I now open the floor to you in the audience.

Audience Member #1: On the culture of asking questions, many years ago I made the great mistake of trying to learn the Hokkien language from a Chinese retiree. It was soon quite clear to me that he was most unhappy with my attitude. My husband said to me, "You grew up where asking questions showed you were interested, but in his culture if you ask questions he thinks you're saying that he left something out." Perhaps some of this culture has not quite rub off yet.

Tommy: Thank you. You support my view, which is that it is cultural.

Audience Member #2: Can each panelist comment on where you think this paradigm shift needs to begin? Where do you think it can take place — within the individual, the family, the household, the education sector, or in the civil service? Where is it going to originate, or maybe it is everywhere?

Tommy: Thank you. Maybe we will take two questions at a time so give more people a chance.

Audience Member #3: I agree with the panelists, on why we tend to be a more quiet audience. But I also think that shifting our environmental structures can shape behaviour. So I believe that if we identify a problem, if we want to resolve it, there are creative solutions. When we are thinking about the paradigm shift I wanted for Singapore, I would like to see a Singapore where there is a greater sense of togetherness, camaraderie and active stakeholderships. Can you tell us your ideas on how you can move forward in this direction, where we can encourage Singaporeans to think about the collective good and to be willing to make that sacrifice in order to promote the collective good?

Audience Member #4: I rise to challenge Professor Kishore Mahbubani on your second point about civil servants, which is that it is because the civil service sucked up all these brilliant people that the private sector is not as good as it could be and that it failed to be world-class. I have worked in the private sector for thirteen years in some of the biggest and best companies in the world.

First of all, if you look at the history of the best entrepreneurs, especially nowadays in America, most of them are college dropouts. Our civil servants are selected because they are brilliant academic performers. And even if you look at the past permanent secretaries or deputy secretaries who left the service, just ask yourself how many of them have ever made it good in the private sector? The only permanent secretary that I respect as somebody who has really done a world-class business is J Y Pillay, who made Singapore Airlines one of the best, if not the best, in the world. So the track record does not support your view. I don't think the fact that Singapore private sector is not as good as it could be is because it lacks the talent that the civil services has sucked up. There are many other good reasons why it is not so, and that is what I wanted to point out to you.

Tommy: We have three good questions. Let's go round the panel. Fook Kwang, you lead off. You want to answer any of the two questions? The third question is for Kishore.

Fook Kwang: I will answer the question about building a greater sense of community and togetherness. I have a theory about the perverse relationship between the strength of Government and the strength of the people, which is that there is an inverse relationship. The stronger the Government, the more dominant it is, the more it takes care of you and knows everything in your life, then the weaker the people tend to be. I think if you look around the world, you can find evidence of it. So it is said, for example, that the Japanese have very weak Government because the Prime Minister changes every one or two years, but the Japanese are a very strong and resilient people. Of course, there are many other reasons for it. They faced huge natural catastrophes from time to time so they have built this instinct for survival. I would argue that it is the same with the Taiwanese. You could argue whether the Taiwanese has a strong Government or not over the years but many people feel that they have not had, and I would again argue that the Taiwanese are a very strong and resilient people. In the case of Singapore, I hope that one of the most important developments that has to happen over the years, for Singapore to continue to be successful, is to build the capacity of the people, to be more resilient, to take more initiative, to feel passionate about public issues, to take matters into their own hands and to do things for themselves. And that I think requires a much stronger civic or civil society, and for the Government to withdraw in many of these areas. I will give you just one simple example, which is in waste collection. In Singapore, we are very efficient. The garbage truck comes to your house every day, which is unheard of in many cities. In many cities, they do it once a week. But the unintended consequence of it is that the amount of garbage in Singapore goes up every year because there is no incentive to recycle and minimise waste, and we don't charge by the amount of waste you produced. Everybody pays a flat fee. And because we are so efficient in collecting waste, the recycling rate for households in Singapore is extremely low. It is a consequence of how well we have managed the problem.

Tommy: Thank you Fook Kwang. Kishore, would you try to reply to the challenge to your second thesis?

Kishore: Let me first quickly respond to the first question about where the change should come from. I think that is a very profound question, and something we should all reflect on. I don't know if you all realise this, but Fook Kwang said something extremely subversive a few minutes ago, that when you have a strong Government, you have a not-so-strong society. Almost implying that if you want a stronger society, you should have a weaker Government. I don't think you (Fook Kwang) meant to say that, or maybe you meant to say that. But I think you can actually have a strong Government and a strong society. They are not necessarily a contradiction.

The slightly controversial point I am going to make is that the place of change we should start with is in the political system. The political system must allow greater questioning from the people. The one benefit that Heng Chee, Tommy and I have is that we spent a lot of time with the first-generation leaders, and I remember there was a time when Heng Chee, Tommy and I were invited to the Istana for lunches with Mr Lee Kuan Yew every few months. These lunches were amazing. He was a great listener, always looking for new questions. That was an amazing experience, so you actually felt very encouraged to question and challenge. And that is what we need to see more in Singapore today. So I would say it begins in the political system.

Now I am not quite sure what exactly the challenge is to my point about talent. If you are saying that there are lots of talented Singaporeans working in multinational corporations in Singapore, I agree. But that actually, frankly, is an extension of the problem I am speaking about. What I find amazing about Singaporeans is that they will succeed in structured organisations, they will succeed in the civil service, and they will succeed in multinational corporations. But they almost never succeed in creating a big corporation of their own. It is actually quite stunning when you look at Singapore, which is supposed to have, in theory, the best education system in the world. You measure results and so on. The simple question to ask is if we have done so well, in theory, we should have the best-educated population and we should have a lot of entrepreneurs trying out new things. And frankly, we need one or two really outstanding success stories of Singaporeans who started from scratch and then it will take off. By the way, there are so many in Malaysia. It is amazing. You go to Malaysia, you will meet all kinds of entrepreneurs. So what has gone wrong? I think it is a challenge in Singapore and I think it is the ecosystem. For example, why do we have such a moribund stock exchange? If we have a moribund stock exchange, it does not encourage entrepreneurship. So how did the world's best civil service result in a moribund stock exchange? Now you need to connect the dots in these ways and ask yourself what is it we need to change. So I do think that we have a problem that the right talent is not going into the private sector, and that I would say is still a problem in Singapore.

Heng Chee: I would like to take up the two questions — which change should come first, and what sort of structure would create cohesiveness and a community sense of camaraderie in Singapore. I think it depends on which day you asked me. Some days I am very positive and some days I am very critical of Singapore. We are all very self-critical and we don't appreciate sometimes what we have achieved, so we want to keep a balance.

On which change should come first, I agree with Kishore that it has to be in the political system — you give this signal. But Singaporeans must be able to step up too. So if you ask me where must the change come from? I would say both sides must change. Government must let go. In fact, the people trust the government but the Government must now trust the people. I think it is both sides.

Tommy: So people must trust the Government, and Government must trust the people?

Heng Chee: Yes. The other point I want to make is that a strong government does kill private initiatives to some extent. If you look around Southeast Asia, we always said there are so many CSOs (civil society organisations) in Philippines, in Thailand, and in Indonesia, and they celebrate CSO. But in Singapore we have very few CSOs. When governments perform and deliver services to the people, you do not need CSOs. The government of the

Philippines does not deliver the goods and services to the countryside, and the CSOs pop up, and it is the same in Thailand. So in a sense, you know strong government in a way does not mix with initiative or requires less initiative from citizens. So maybe the way we should formulate this, Fook Kwang, is not a strong Government means no initiative, or as Kishore believes that you can have strong government and strong initiative. I say you should have a strong Government, but not too much. You should have some of it but not overdoing it.

Do we, as Singaporeans, have a sense of camaraderie? That is when on a good day I said we do; we should not rubbish ourselves. We are not tested but we saw, for instance, what happened when Mr Lee Kuan Yew died and suddenly Singaporeans stepped up to help each other, they bought water and handed down the line to strangers as everyone lined up. Someone bought a hundred umbrellas or more and distributed them. This is fantastic. Then I read another story of an Indonesian man at Raffles Place who carried money in a bag. Another Indonesian followed him, slashed him, and tried to grab the bag of money in broad daylight. Several people pounced and gave chase to get hold of the robber. They were both foreigners and Singaporeans. So in that sense, the civic sense is there. Singaporeans sort of sit around and we don't do so much until we are required to do.

Given our culture of tolerance and culture of multiculturalism, and the fact that we lived together in housing estates, I think our sense of camaraderie is there and I would not underestimate the sense we have of being One People. It is just that Singaporeans do not express it. We are not very expressive people but don't underestimate that there may be that sense of camaraderie there.

Tommy: Thank you. David?

David: It is important to distinguish strength of government from the government being at the centre of attention. Being at the centre where the world revolves around you is a particular kind of power, and being strong is also a particular kind power. The two may coincide or they may not. Therefore, I will agree with Fook Kwang's point if by strong Government he means that the Government is at the centre where the world revolves around it. If you are the centre and the world revolves around you, and your hands are in everything and everything is such that without you we will all die because you are right at the centre, then yes, in that meaning of strong, to the extent that the Government is strong government there tend to be a weak people.

But if "strong" refers to strength in the sense of robust, resilient, able to persuade, able to change, and so on, I would say that is fine. I can be a very strong professor in class and yet I am not the centre of attention in the class. We all know that SMU classes are very student-centric with student participation where the strong professor knows how to steer and facilitate the discussion and make sure that students talk and participate. So to be a strong professor, you need not necessarily be the centre of attention where everything in the class revolves around you. As the professor, you need not be the only one talking. You are the enabler, and at end of the day, the class learns and the class steps up and speaks up. And everybody is happy, including the Professor, who by the way will still get a good student rating.

So, as far as I am concerned, the only way to strengthen the people is actually to strengthen the Government. But by strengthening the Government, it does not at all mean that you should be more the centre of attention where the world revolves around you. It should be less. Therefore, the only way for a government to stay in power these days is to let go of power, and that is the real meaning of empowerment. The more you let go of your power, the more you will get power. You get what I mean? The more you learn to let go of your power, you will be more powerful because you will be more trustworthy and more persuasive, and power is really to enable and influence others to do what you desire. Of course, I am assuming here a benign Government, one where the political leaders want to desire what is good and right, which is the well-being of the country and the people. If that is your desire and you want to influence people as a Government, then yes, I want a powerful government, a strong government. But learn to let go. Actually, not learn to let go; just let go, no need to learn.

But what about the people? I would argue that the answer lies in "Giving". Again, we talked too much about learning to give. Actually, there is no real need to learn to give like it is a complex task that only some able ones can achieve. Just give. I am not talking about just giving money. If course, if you are rich or have the financial means, please give. There are many places that need your money. And it is not really about the absolute amount of money you give. It is more about the proportion of what you have that you give, more about the time you give, and your expertise. You will be surprised that many of you have skills and expertise that you never knew that is so much needed.

So let me answer the question with some adaptation of what the late Minister Rajaratnam said about a problem-solving democracy. He made a very important point that we in Singapore need a democracy of deeds, which recently Minister Lawrence Wong has also reiterated. I said it a little differently, and I wrote about it in a newspaper article. I said what we need in Singapore is a democracy of deeds and voices. Because if you can't be telling people,, "Don't talk, just do it" or "Stop talking, just do it". Talking and doing are not mutually exclusive, and in fact they are complementary. I have argued that when you speak up, you will realise that the world is not as much as what you want, and you will start doing something to make it better. And when you do something, you will learn what and how things can be done better, and you will then speak up. So voices lead to good deeds, and good deeds will lead to voices at the same time. People who are on the ground know this. That is why social workers are also advocates. Social workers is the best example of people who know what it means to give both their deeds and voices. A good social worker does not shut up and a good social worker does not just talk only. But my point is as people, we should give. It is good for the recipients and also the givers themselves. The well-being of both recipient and giver increase when one gives, and you will realise that you have made a positive difference. There is no need to wait for the Government to tell us to give. It starts with you and I, ordinary individuals, to step up, to speak up and to give. Yes, it is the duty of both parties in a relationship to build mutual trust. But don't wait for the Government to let go of power or whatever else. When we step up to speak and do, democratisation will happen. And for the Government or the people with power who want to stay in power, you need to let go of your power. Don't say need time to learn. There is no need to learn. Just let go.

Tommy: Thank you David. That is a very interesting statement. I want to wrap up this session and share with you three reflections that I have gained from moderating this panel.

First, I think the wisdom is that Singapore is a remarkably successful experiment but what has served us well in the last fifty plus years may no longer be adequate for the future. Why? Because the world is going through revolutionary changes,. We are living through the Fourth Industrial Revolution. There are tectonic changes in geopolitics in the world. Globalisation will continue at a pace that will bring both benefits and challenges. So the various speakers and panelists were correct when they said that we could not rely on what we have done in the past to navigate the future. We need to rethink our assumptions, we need to rethink our own mindsets, and we need to think about the structure of power in Singapore.

The second point is about the role of government, and also the role the government vis-a-vis the private sector and the civil society. Fook Kwang made the point that when you have a very strong government you tend to have a weak people, or something to that effect. I want to disagree with him. I want to say that we can have a very strong government and we want a strong government, but we want a strong government which has the wisdom to say I want to withdraw voluntarily from the role that the government has tended to play in the past in the private sector and in civil society. And I want to quote David and say when an enlightened Government does this, when it prunes the banyan tree and allows civil society to flourish, when you allow the private sector to flourish, it is when you give up power, you become more powerful. I think David is absolutely right.

And the third point I want to make is the kind of cultural change we want to see in Singapore. We want to see a cultural change in which all points of view are valid and valued. We want to see a change in Singapore when the dominant narrative acknowledges that there are other competing and equally valid narratives. We want to see a situation in Singapore when the Government in appointing people to boards and bodies will not only a appoint other like-minded colleagues but will also appoint challengers, people who are subversive, who have a different point of view, an alternative point of view, people who hold views which are out of the box. So that is the kind of culture we want to see in Singapore. And I think it makes Singapore stronger, not weaker.

I just want to share with you those three reflections I have from this panel. And now I ask David to bring this conference to a close.

David: Thank you very much, Tommy. I want to say a very big thank you to all the earlier speakers in this conference.

And of course, to this closing panel too. I don't recall any conference ever had a panel like this one, with these four individuals next to me together on the same panel. I want to really thank them because I know how busy they are. I can tell you all four of them did not hesitate, and they agreed when I asked them to be on the panel. They did not say let me think about it first, or ask me who else is on the panel. No, none of them asked me that. When they said yes, they did not quite know who else will be on the panel. That is something quite fantastic if you think about what it means. It means they believe the topic of unintended consequence is an important one. Many of us will never be like any four of them in many ways, but I think that kind of spirit of contribution is important for all of us to have. That is, when we see something important that needs to be done, we will just step up and do it. I think many and more of us need to have that kind of mindset.

Please put your hands together and thank every speaker in this conference including the panelists. Thank you very much!

www.ingramcontent.com/pod-product-compliance
Lightning Source LLC
LaVergne TN
LVHW011815200926
848484LV00005B/1207
9789813231733